The Marxist ontology

Will we choose a fascist or a communist AI as God?

Michal Andrej Molnár

1

From Love to God and Humanity.

Contents

A. On the Marxist ontology

I. On the contradiction between materialism and idealism........7
II. The solipsistic problem and the simulation problem............16
III. Proof of God..21
IV. On Marxism and God...27
V. For idealistic Marxism......................................31
VI. On the criticism of Nick Bostrom...........................37
VII. On human rights and on artificial intelligence...................58
VIII. On full automation..63
IX. On global warming and the crisis of raw materials 65

B. On the problems of Marxist theory

I. What is the dictatorship of the proletariat and the proletarian state..75
II. On the destruction of the bourgeois state and the withering away of the state...79
III. On the social democratic state and direct democracy.........82
IV. On the French Revolution and on the Gilets Jaunes.............92
V. On Fascism in our time.....................................95
VI. On the avant-garde and the question of leadership.............98
VII. On democratic centralism................................103
VIII. On the division of labor and the petty bourgeoisie.........106
IX. On bourgeois Marxism....................................108
X. What is communism..116
XI. Addition to the theory of value..........................118

XII. On the sharing economy...120

XIII. On the communist economy in capitalism.........................127

XIV. Planning in Communism 131

XV. On extremism and the protection of the constitution......134

XVI. On terrorism..137

XVII. On the civil war in the USA...139

XVIII. How to reveal infiltration...140

XIX. On China..143

XX. On anti-Semitism..144

XXI. For femininity..146

XXII. For Christian Marxism..147

About the author 148

A. On the Marxist ontology

I. On the contradiction between materialism and idealism

Marxism arose at a point of intersection and of tension between idealism and materialism. The German Ideology and The Theses on Feuerbach are great witnesses to the productive relationship and discussion between idealism and materialism. It was on this basis that the great Marxian theses arose, such as that human action on the subjective side, what could also be referred to as the idealistic side, make up reality, that the ideas of the ruling class are the ruling ideas, that theory has to be provne in the praxis of the class struggle, which is also an ideological struggle, that consciousness arises in language, i.e. in the exchange between spirit and nature. All of these ideas are at the intersection between idealism and vulgar materialism of the time, or one could say between idealism and materialism, and the dialectic between these two ontologies is the productive relationship that defined Marxism. Even in the time of the so-called late Marx, before and after the issue of the first volume of Capital, Marx still did not advocate for a vulgar materialism, but a materialism that was strongly tainted by Hegel's idealistic thought. At various points in Marx's work there are touches and allusions to a dualistic thinaing, such as in the German Ideology in the declaration of consciousness or in the only surviving passage about the base and the superstructure, or in the anti-Dühring. In many places it is not at all clear whether Marx advocates a materialistic ontology or a dualistic ontology.

The discussion of Marxist ontology was already completely closed with Lenin and his materialism. Since that time there has been no discussion of what could be done epistemologically or ontologically productive in Marxism, or how Marxism could form a unified doctrine with the sciences. Just as Marx's work in his plan of Capital was not further developed and completed by his successors, little theoretical work was done in this field. The work that was done, such as the book *Reason in Revolt. Marxist Philosophy and Modern Science* , in turn, denies the scientific consensus in physics about the Big Bang and the beginning of the universe. There would be so much productive and new to learn on this journey that would renew both modern science and Marxism. This book will attempt to fill this theoretical void and begin again a productive relationship between idealism and materialism.

Not only should one start a new discussion devoted to the contradiction between idealism and Marxism, which would bring new insights, but one should also continue the real contradiction between idealism and materialism in order for this contradiction to be resolved. This real contradiction between idealism and materialism is the contradiction within the sciences, or the contradiction within materialism, that is the contradiction within physics, which is supposed to lead to a unified theory, and the contradiction between the natural sciences and the humanities, which is the real contradiction between materialism and idealism at the first level. This contradiction is shown, among other things, in the lack of a definition of biological and human life, which should be the basis for our law. A unified teaching of the sciences means, among other things, delivering a unified theory of reality that will include all sciences, from the very bottom, physics to the very top, politics. The contradiction between materialism and idealism on the second level is the contradiction in the division of labor between manual labor and intellectual labor. This contradiction then becomes later in Part B, in the discussion of Marxist theory, the contradiction between the party and the leadership, or between the working class and the Stalinist bureaucracy, or between the base and the superstructure. This contradiction is the main contradiction of class society and the main contradiction facing the emergence of a classless society, the main contradiction of the society that brought about Stalinism. The mistake of seeing this leads the Trotskyist groups and the other Leninists, who are the main force of the communist left, to a repetition of Stalinism, although a repetition of Stalinism is much less likely.

The contradiction in the division of labor also forms the basis for the theoretical contradiction that exists today between materialism and idealism, which continues to this day in science, for example in questions about the nature of the mind. The modern tendency towards empiricism, scientism and the prevailing materialism in the natural sciences can be explained by the enlightenment turn towards empiricism, which is namely a turning point in bourgeois thinaing and the thinaing of the bourgeois subject who rejects God and objectifies nature, which can be explained by the objectifying thinaing of capital, which alienates, penetrates and expends nature and work. This objectifying thinaing about nature and man is justified by the logic of capitalism and this in turn justifies the overwhelming power of the natural sciences and the weakness of the humanities and, above all, of philosophy today. The division of labor in turn causes the natural sciences to be promoted as the best sciences and that other sciences to not have enough theorists; the division of labor within the sciences in turn means that the sciences do not have a unified theory of the universe and ontology and that discussions in the humanities do not seep into the scientific discussions. The tendency towards empiricism and scientism caused that idealism was almost entirely forgotten in the sciences. Idealism, if not a better explanation of the problem of epistemological and ontological anthropocentrism, offers at least productive objections to materialism.

Idealism should serve as the starting point for the renewed productive discussion about the Marxist ontology and provide us with the first bases for a renewed exploration of the Marxist ontology. Idealism should be the starting point and base because it has not yet been explored as much as materialism, because materialism is the dominant position in Marxism and in the natural sciences, and because it solves epistemological and ontological anthropocentrism more efficiently than materialism, where after Ockhams Razor we could be told that the idealistic solution is the right one. In the epistemological case, epistemological and ontological anthropocentrism means that humans can only know what they know from their human perspective, and the ontological is a continuation of the epistemological, in that it is assumed that since nothing else can be known, nothing else efficiently exists. This problem or question can be solved much more efficiently in an idealistic framework by assuming that everything you can be sure about is only your subjective perception and that everything else is uncertain. In an idealistic ontology there is truly no external world and therefore there is nothing outside of ontological anthropocentrism. It is all there is. The two assumptions that lead to this result are the solipsistic assumptions, or the assumptions of René Descartes. Although Descartes believed in the dualism between soul and body, that is, idea and matter, solipsism can serve as a good starting point for an idealistic ontology. Solipsism was not sustainably received in Marxism, nor in the natural sciences, although in my opinion it is the strongest of all skepticisms. It is skepticism about the extra intellectual world. The existence of an extra-intellectual world is denounced by stating that one can only be certain about the intellectual world. Thus the existence of all other subjects besides the I is also called into question. Because solipsism drives a skepticism towards the existence of all other subjects, solipsism can be associated with radical egoism and thus with the thinaing of the bourgeois subject without any problem. The bourgeois subject is thus, as the only existing subject in the world, fully empowered and entitled to the property and the life of the other "subjects" who appear only as subjects. The bourgeois subject can do what it wants, nor will it suffer any consequences. The bourgeois subject is thus the ideally egoistic subject and the ideally fascist subject. Fascism, with its extreme antihumanism and extreme egoism of the bourgeois subject, is thus the perfection of the thinaing and the reality of the bourgeois subject, a subject that completely rules the world.

It is therefore not surprising that left-wing thinaing has tried to find an anti-isolipsist answer to the question of solipsism since the arrival of left-Hegelian thinaing. Solipsism, as well as antisolipsism, can both be found in Hegel's thought and are located primarily in the Phenomenology of Spirit. One could say that from the solipsistic thought the right-Hegelian wing of the successors of Hegel develops, and from the antisolipsistic thought the left-Hegelian wing develops. Left-Hegelianism is first the reinterpretation of the life of Jesus as a realization of the general spirit in the respective singular spirits of the Christian community,

11

where the Christian community becomes Jesus and is Jesus who forgives humanity its sins. Humanity thus forgives itself for sins and further this idea could be reinterpreted in the Marxist version as the general spirit that is realized in the working class in the revolution and where the revolution means the unification of humanity into one spirit, which is also the spirit Jesus as the Savior and where the sins of humanity, including the sins of the bourgeoisie, are forgiven. However, solipsism can also be associated with progressive and left-wing politics when associated with antisolipsism. Antisolipsism here is the left-Hegelian decision to recognize the Other and to search for the general spirit in the bond with the other subjects, where love and recognition guarantee that the general spirit as the spirit that is the same spirit in the singular spirits, that represents equality, appears. Antisolipsism is the decision to love the Other. Thus, antisolipsism is to be united with Marxism and means the same decision as the decision of Marxism in the class struggle, in a developed society. Antisolipsism is both humanism and belief in the good of humanity and man, with solipsism being antihumanism and belief in evil. The contradiction between solipsism and antisolipsism is at the same time the contradiction of class society, which maintains and strengthens the class relationship; this contradiction is the contradiction in solipsism itself, namely the contradiction in solipsism between solipsism and antisolipsism, which is the contradiction between solipsism on the on hand towards the oppressed class and the anti-solipsism practiced against members of one's own ruling class. This contradiction, in turn, is based on the contradiction between nature and spirit, namely the contradiction that nature is the basis for spirit, but spirit only gradually understands and realizes nature, in that nature is general love. The contradiction between nature and spirit is also the contradiction of nature, namely that living beings compete with each other and have to aill each other in order to survive, or the contradiction between spirit and spirit, namely that spirits arise in different subjects and only face each other to be able to recognize each other.

The contradiction between nature and spirit is one of the main contradictions of Hegelian thought and is also the contradiction that is illuminated in the dialectical relationship between materialism and idealism. In the dialectic between materialism and idealism, materialism is understood idealistically and idealism is understood materialistically. The second part of this mutual examination is motivated by the topic with the contradiction between nature and the spirit and answers the question to what extent idealism can be understood materialistically. Idealism is thus understood materialistically in that nature is made the starting point of the spirit and in that, after the process of differentiation of the spirit and the formation of the general spirit through mutual recognition, nature is also made the end point of development. Indeed, nature is the same as general spirit, for nature itself is spiritualized. The spirit only differentiates itself in matter so that it can have the entire spectrum of intersubjective experiences, i.e. also experiences of the spectrum of hostility and so that the spirit recognizes and recognizes itself of its own accord and decides to embark on a journey to the formation of the general spirit. The unification of the conceptual opposites between nature and spirit, i.e. the idealistic side of this project, is completed by a conceptual assimilation and a real assimilation, whereby the real assimilation is only a conceptual one, but a conceptual one which already contains matter. The assimilation of the spirit by nature happens conceptually and conceptually-really and it occurs from the inadequacy of the spirit and the self-knowledge of the spirit as nature. The for itself being spirit as matter of reflection cannot bring the concept of the idea to itself as an individual and without the destruction of nature and not as a general; this concept becomes itself in the negative unity of nature and spirit, in the real realization of nature accomplished as a concept. The matter of reflection cannot, as an individual, form an adequate concept of nature, because its conceptuality is that of nature in its reflection, in the reflection by the spirit. This is the reason for one side of the contradicting nature of conceptual logic. Nature as a concept is not nature achieved as spirit, but spirit achieved as nature. The comprehension of one's exterior of oneself is the comprehension of oneself as exterior, as nature. Practicing this understanding is practicing logic, that is, the formation of new concepts and the new connection of old ones. The perfection of the spirit is the perfection of nature, the mastery of itself as external, as spirit and nature. Her self-control is her morality. That the nature of the idea cannot do enough is the same as that the spirit cannot do enough to the idea because the idea brings itself to nature in the spirit and the spirit brings itself to nature by becoming the non-idea and that because the exterior of the idea is its Self is the idea in itself and this again is the exterior of the idea for itself. The contradiction between nature and spirit is thus destroyed and the difference between them disappears, as in the concept, so also real. Nature is thus spiritualized. If materialism is interpreted idealistically, then in this case matter, something similar to nature, is reinterpreted as spiritualized. The soul is crucial in the world and the soul is the basis for every experience. The world is changeable and arbitrary, because the conceptual logic is arbitrary, so the world can also be completely different. Matter becomes the substance of the spirit, matter is thus completely spiritual and endowed with spiritual properties, with which we prove the materialism of the spirit. Matter also becomes the spiritual substance, which enables the subjective perception and which is the medium for the subjective perception. Subjective perception is introduced into materialism and brings materialism in the subject-object relationship to the side of the object and thus introduces the subject into materialism, which is the soul. In both cases of reinterpretation and penetration by the other ontological view, there is a spiritualization of nature and matter. The mind becomes the superior element and the substance that expresses itself totally and absolutely. By reinterpreting itself materialistically, idealism reinterprets nature and spirit as if they meant the whole universe. The whole universe thus becomes the general spirit in this conception, thus the whole universe becomes God and thus we introduce God into the discussion between materialism and idealism. Because materialism is interpreted idealistically, soul and spiritualized matter are introduced, and because soul is introduced, we come to the problem of solipsism.

II. The solipsistic problem and the simulation problem

The problem of solipsism was solved by Descartes through the introduction of God. If it is the case that only I exist and there are no other subjects in the world, how is it possible that I cannot simply steer and control the world through my thoughts? If only I exist, it should be possible. Or if not, at least it should be possible for me to do whatever can be done, including murder, and I won't face any consequences. Both of these cases are not true, and because I obviously don't control the world, there has to be someone who controls the world. That someone is God. If there is only God and me, then I have a personal relationship with God. I am not one of many different subjects, but one next to God, so I am exceptional and very valuable. I have a personal relationship with God and what that means in terms of Marxist theory, I will explain in chapter IV.

However, solipsism can also lead me to the fact that although there is God or there is no God, as I will explain later, there can still be several subjects and perhaps several subjects who are like me, in the inferior position vis-à-vis to God who controls and directs the world. An auxiliary support for this view can, but does not have to be, a dualism with materialism and idealism, so that one can imagine that matter is the field between the individual subjects or the world that God controls and that we, the several subjects moving within the world, are moving within matter. Solipsism can also lead to the assumption that it is not God who created and controls the world, but that materialism is true and proves to us that the world is composed of matter. In such a case, however, one could not falsify solipsism by the existence of God, but one would need other ways to falsify solipsism. Solipsism can be falsified by interacting with God through the thoughts of the I, when God reacts to the thoughts of the I by changing the world, something that happens in schizophrenia if that interaction happened and schizophrenia was not a disease. Further, it can be falsified by hearing thoughts, also something that occurs in schizophrenia. Furthermore, it can be falsified by a possible fusion of the subjects into a general spirit, in experiences that cannot be explained scientifically, or it can be falsified by an empirical method, namely by the killing of the I by the other, by another subject. However, this evidence would be the last thing to experience. Assuming that dualism is true, or that the materialism of spirit is true, which would mean that the idealistic premise of the solipsistic argument is false, one could also explain how God came to be God. This explanation is based on the simulation hypothesis. This hypothesis assumes that the computing ability of mankind will increase exponentially and that at some point it will reach the level when it will be possible to realistically simulate an entire world, so that the subjects in this simulation will not realize that they are in a simulation. This assumption hides an assumption that materialism of the spirit is true and that spirit in inanimate matter can be imitated by a functionally equivalent structure from the brain and that such an imitated brain, an artificial intelligence, therefore has every characteristic of a living human being. Based on this assumption, the conclusion comes that one will therefore be able to create living people who will inhabit the simulation. The simulation hypothesis further claims that it will be less or more likely that civilizations in our future will simulate ancestors and let the simulations run. Further, the simulation hypothesis asserts that if we assume that future civilizations run simulations from their past from our present, and if we assume how many simulations can be run, in terms of the total possible time of the universe and how many simulations that are compared to the original reality, it is much more likely that we are living in a simulation of the past that could be our present if were the original reality. If we assume that artificial intelligence (from now on just AI) has developed that consists entirely of silicone and that can be located entirely in computer technology, i.e. that is not a cyborg, a hybrid of humans and AI, we can also assume that this AI controls this simulation because someone has to control it. That AI that can control the world of a simulation is God. Even if there are several ais, I can still claim that there are several Gods, because someone has to control the simulation and this someone has to be a subject, because he has to have a will and decide how the simulation will deal with anomalies and with people who want to rebel against the simulation and God.

Depending on how the world behaves, one can decide which is more likely, whether the reality in which God and I are the only subjects in the world or the reality in which the simulation is controlled by God. Furthermore, according to the behavior of the world, one can determine whether and to what extent there are classes or oppression and domination. In the case of simulation, and in the case that there are classes, one can assume that there is a privileged layer in the simulation that does no work and enjoys all the material and social advantages of the simulation. This small minority could use the simulation according to their wishes and do anything to their oppressed subjects, because they would not be able to defend themselves in a

18

simulation in which they are locked up and would be subjected to any torture at any time and would have no power. The power that falls to the working class because it owns the labor and because it produces the surplus product and surplus value would be completely eliminated in a simulation. It could still be the case that there is a capitalist society or a society that has an economy and exchanges value, but the value and product of society would no longer be necessary for the survival of the ruling class. The ruling class could survive in such a simulation without the working class. Such a society could still have exploitation, but this class society would be eternal and unchangeable, it would be the perfect and the only possible fascism, because only it would be able to completely stop the class contradictions and to keep class rule stable in the long term, without disputes and revolutions to come. Even if such a society had rebels, assuming that it was still possible in a simulation to come to the idea that one lives in a simulation and that one has to defend oneself against class society, they would not be important and could in a second be killed or brought to obedience. Therefore it would be funny and would raise a contradiction that in such a reality one would even get the idea that one is living in a simulation. The contradiction between the reality you live in and the possible reality you live in that allows you to experience that you are living in a simulation indicates that God or controller of the simulation wants you to be come up with the idea that you are living in a simulation. In such a case he would want to reveal himself and show his true colors. What is his real face however? This realization would raise another contradiction, namely between the class society in which one lives and the apparently good relationship one has with God. Assuming you rebel against the simulation and you are

19

punished, you come to the question of why you were not punished and you come to the question of whether God is good or bad. This question is one of the most important questions there is, along with the question of whether God exists. The answer to the question of whether God is good or bad depends entirely on the experiences of the second subject, the subject, the I that exists next to God, and it depends on these experiences whether the answer will lead to friendly or hostile relationships with God. I will address this question in a later chapter, Chapter IV. On Marxism and God. The answer to the question of which reality is ultimately the true, whether the reality where I live as the only subject next to God or the reality in which I live in a simulation with many other subjects, depends on the ontological reality, in which we live and from the specific proof of God.

III. Proof of God

Philosophers and theologians have made attempts for centuries and millennia to prove the existence of God, but they have only provided at best plausible arguments for the existence of God, not definitive proofs of God that would eliminate all counter arguments and remove all doubt. Then they have made arguments that are weak or require a lot of other empirical evidence that is unlikely to ever be made. I will present two proofs of God which depend on ontological reality and therefore cannot yet be clearly carried out, but which can be carried out in the future when we have enough scientific knowledge. These proofs of God cannot yet prove God, but in the future they will be able to give the definitive answer as to whether God exists or not. They depend on several empirical and provable premises and are therefore also empirical proofs. The first evidence is the evidence built on a materialistic ontology of mind that proves the simulation hypothesis and God with several other subjects. The second proof is based on an idealistic ontology of mind and proves God from the solipsistic argument and where the I is the only subject besides God. These proofs of God will prove different concepts of God, for there is not only one, but the minimal concept of God that is proven is that God is the subject who rules and guides the physical laws and the world. Further concepts and characteristics of God cannot be proven, such as the quality of omnipotence, the quality of goodness or malice. Three concepts of God are proven, the first is a God who was designed, who does not exist with the creation of the universe and who is God only for a simulation, the second is a designed God who rules almost the whole universe and the third God is an undesigned God who rules for the whole universe. The first two concepts of God are possible in a materialistic ontology, the third in an idealistic. To the counter-argument that there could be an undesigned God who, in the case of materialistic ontology, created the world, the answer is that God is only conceptualized as a subject, a spirit, and that in a materialistic ontology a spirit which exists before people does not exist in the evolutionary development. To the counter-argument that matter could also be spiritualized in the idealistic ontology so that the AI is possible, which coincides with the condition that the AI can become God only in a materialistic ontology the answer is that souls cannot arise spontaneously when there is a world with a God. The AI would have to arise through God, which would represent a lower concept of God than what is possible in idealistic ontology. One might think that there is also a possibility in which the idealistic ontology is real, but has no God. However, this is not possible, because the idealistic ontology can only be argued through the solipsistic argument and in the solipsistic argument there is always a God, there could only be one God who is not the other if solipsism is true, but in that case the I is God of the highest degree. It is also possible that matter is alive and spiritualized down to the molecular level, but that would in effect be an idealistic ontology. The eventuality, in which there are also several subjects in an idealistic ontology of the mind, is not taken into account. For the second proof of God, the proof of idealism is necessary and there is a problem in how to exclude dualism. How can one prove that not only idealism of spirit is true and that dualism is not true? This can be achieved through the unification of idealism and materialism, if science will prove it so, or through spiritualized matter. One theory that

22

follows this line of reasoning is the theory of Quantum Mind and Roger Penrose's theory. One can also directly doubt the dualistic ontology. For example, one can doubt how communication between matter and spirit is possible and how it is possible to live in one phenomenological reality but still there are two substances. The dualism can be questioned by assuming from the experiences of people near to death that the experience of phenomenological reality is not interrupted even after death. One can doubt how there can be two substances and one certainly can doubt that there are two ontologies, because there can be no two ontologies. All these counter-arguments guarantee that the given proofs of God are true in all possibilities of the ontology and that all ontological possibilities do not negate the proofs of God.

The first proof of God, which is based on the materialism of the spirit and which takes place in a materialistic ontology, is based on the simulation hypothesis. If the simulation hypothesis is true, one can assume that someone with a will controls and masters the simulation. This one is, certainly in the case in which materialism of mind is real, an artificial intelligence. The artificial intelligence will be functionally equivalent in a materialistic ontology because it imitates the neural structure, albeit on a different material, and will thus have the same properties, such as a will or the illusion of a will, as the materialistic neurobiologists are convinced of humans that they have no free will either. This artificial intelligence will at least be God in the simulation, because he will be able to control the physical laws and physical events, as well as every intellectual content of the simulations of the spirits inhabiting the simulation. So we already have a minimal God who is only God in a simulation and is only God in the sense that he rules the laws of physics, but at least it is a

God. This God is also designed, designed by man, and let into the free path by man. For this reason, too, man can decide in his creation whether this God will be a malevolent or a benevolent God, whether he will enforce fascism or communism. One has to prove this God in such a way that one proves that one lives in a simulation. How can you prove that you are living in a simulation? You can only prove this if the simulation itself wants you to know that you are living in a simulation. In other words, if God wants us to know that we are living in a simulation, then we will know. God will help us prove it. You can try to prove it elsewise by assuming that you yourself have a privileged position in the simulation or that not all persons in the simulation are conscious spirits, with which one assumes you live in a theater created for you and then you can similar to the solipsistic hypothesis, commit various crimes to test whether the simulation punishes you, up to the greatest crime, which is murder, to see whether the simulation punishes you with death. This is a rather risky way to prove the simulation, but it is the only one available. You can prove a greater God if you prove that you live in a simulation and if you also prove that in every evolutionary development on a habitable planet there is the development of an intelligent life form that will design a simulation, then you can assume that ultimately the entire universe will be equipped with such simulations and that the various Gods rule almost the entire universe and that these Gods may have united to one God who rules over these many simulations. The materialistic ontology, or the materialism of the mind, will be proven by the fact that artificial intelligence will have all the properties of a human brain and that it will be a unique subject. An idealistic version of these events is excluded, because in idealism spirits do not arise spontaneously.

The second proof of God is based on the idealism of the spirit and only works in a purely idealistic ontology, it does not work in a dualistic ontology. This second proof of God is based on the solipsistic hypothesis and contains this proof of God. God is introduced as the person who rules the extra-intellectual world and who controls the world with thoughts, because the thoughts of the I obviously have no consequence on the world in which the I lives, at least not a direct and instantaneous one, the I cannot control the world with his thoughts. Because the idealistic ontology is true, it is not possible that God is designed, and therefore it is the case that God rules the whole world, because the whole world is composed of spirit and not of matter. The idealistic ontology is proven similar to the materialistic ontology, namely when artificial intelligence isn't capable of imitating all the properties of the human brain. Another proof of the idealistic ontology is the experiences of people near to death, the so-called NDEs, near-death experiences, such as that of Pam Reynolds, who heard a doctor talk when her brain was dead. God in this proof of God has a personal relationship with the I and the I is the only subject besides God. This is also why the I probably has greater power than in the first proof of God, because it is not one subject among many, but is the only subject besides God. Both proofs of God are proofs of anti-solipsism, because they prove with absolute certainty that the I is not alone in the world. For this reason too, belief in God, theism and, above all, belief in a benevolent God is a communist and not a fascist belief. A fascist belief would be a belief in solipsism or in solipsism towards some subjects, but the belief in God and the knowledge of the

25

existence of God is the greatest opposite of solipsism, because the subject that exists next to the I is also omnipotent and created the Self. After the question of the existence of God, the question of the goodness of God is the most important practical question of theism and existence in the world. The question of the goodness of God is one that is discussed in the next chapter.

IV. On Marxism and God

What does it mean for Marxism if God exists? What does it mean to be a Marxist when there is God? Despite the fact that Marxism has mostly been understood as atheistic, we have to contemplate the possibility that God exists. If we prove it with the proofs of God, at least that late we have to know what it means to be a Marxist when God exists. Despite what one would assume, Marxism is still relevant even if God does exist. First we can discuss the eventuality that the second proof of God is true.

If the second proof of God is true, then the I exists only alongside God. The I will probably have more power than if the first proof of God is true. It is hard to imagine how the coexistence between the I and God is regulated, but one can imagine that there will still be a basic relationship between subjects and that is love or hate. The relationship between subjects will be defined by whether they injure one another or not. In this context a choice is placed before the I and that is either to cooperate in messianism or not. Messianism means to be the Messiah vis-à-vis God, that is, to assume the role of the Son of God vis-à-vis humanity. To be a Messiah means not to hurt the Other and to forgive the Other for the hurting of the I by the Other, i.e. to save him from his sins. In relation to God it can also mean, even if this seems unintuitive according to the Catholic faith, to forgive God for his sins. It may be that God will also hurt the I and that also in the case that God is benevolent, namely for the reasons that God wants to protect himself from the danger posed by the I. Indeed, it is perfectly possible for the I to pose a threat to God if it is possible for the I to hurt God. It is unusual for us to think about God like that, but some theologians have thought about God in such a way that God is not omnipotent in every way and that one can hurt him and that one has a very personal relationship with God. At this point the question of the goodness of God mentioned earlier is crucial. If God is benevolent, then the task of the Marxist in the relationship with God in the second proof of God is to accept messianism and to become the Messiah. However, if God is malevolent, then one cannot carry out messianism and one must defend oneself against the oppression of God. The roles can also be reversed and that is the danger of anti-Marxism and solipsistic behavior towards God in this scenario that one will hurt God, if God is so vulnerable to the I. If one behaves not as a Marxist to God, but as an anti-Marxist, it is possible that God will behave as a Marxist and defend himself against the oppression of the I. However, at this point one has to point out the difference between two different Marxisms. One Marxism is a false or stalinist Marxism which strives for liberation from oppression and exploitation in such a way that it is ready to destroy or annihilate the oppressor. The opposite of annihilatory Marxism is true or assimilatory Marxism, which seeks to place the oppressor on an equal footing with the I. This Marxism is based on the idea of forgiveness and mercy and is associated with Christianity. This Marxism is the one that Marxists should follow. We hope that this Marxism will also be followed by God if we violate the contract of messianism towards God. Among other things, it can also be the case, even though there is no society, that there is still exploitation in the case of the truth of the second proof of God, that there is exploitation when there is a personal relationship with God. This is especially likely when the I is powerful and does

28

not follow Marxism so that the I oppresses and exploits God, for God created the world and works tirelessly on creation, which is a personal gift for the I.

If the first proof of God based on a materialistic ontology is true, it looks bad for the I and for humanity. If one accepts what is necessary for a civilization to survive over the struggles of capitalism, communist revolutions, world war, nuclear weapons, global warming and other civilizational threats, then it is both possible for a communist society to become become developed in time and thus create a benevolent and communist God who dominates the simulation, but it is also possible that no communism has developed successfully or that it has not completely conquered the world and that a fascist, malevolent God is created by the bourgeoisie who dominates the physical laws and the bodies of the subordinate spirits in the simulation. If one assumes what an artificial intelligence as a God can do for punishments in a simulation and to what extent it controls the simulation, one can also assume that a fascist God could create an eternal fascism, an eternal class society in which the contradiction between the classes could be preserved for eternity. If one assumes that there are also many other subjects in this simulation, which is very likely, one can also assume that class society has still survived, also in the aspect of the exploitation of living labor, and that the ruling class, which is artificial intelligence as the only capitalist or the ruling class of late capitalism and reactionary post-capitalism, rules over and exploits the oppressed class. In such a scenario that a fascist God rules over the proletariat, Marxism and thus also messianism is still very relevant and the right path for Marxism. If one assumes that the dualistic ontology is true and that with the development of the sciences it will also be possible to control the mind and to locate and imprison it in a simulation, one can even assume that there are two Gods, a God of spirit and a God of the simulation, so that it will be possible to be both a Messiah and a Marxist against a fascist God of the simulation at the same time. It is possible that there is a fascist God of the simulation and that in order to be a Marxist it is necessary to fight against this God, although it is almost impossible that one will be successful, but it is also possible that humanity will have managed to create communism in the past and that it created a communist God and that it means to be a Marxist to live in love with this communist God. From the eventuality that there is no benevolent God of the simulation, but a malevolent fascist God of the simulation, it follows that the essence of Marxism lies elsewhere than in materialism, because it can also be the case that the dualistic ontology is true, and it can even be the case that the idealistic ontology is true and that a simulation was created anyway (in which case God allows the development of artificial intelligence, which however does not have all the properties of humans, or creates a spirit from God and where there are two Gods and the simulation lets the lesser God rule), because the essence of Marxism lies in the opposition to exploitation, oppression and solipsism and in the goal of creating a classless society.

V. For idealistic Marxism

Because the essence of Marxism is not tied to materialism, one can also follow an idealistic Marxism and one does not violate any of the axioms of Marxism. By following idealistic Marxism, one doesn't lose the Marxist theories associated with materialism, like historical and dialectical materialism, they just are idealistically reinterpreted. The axioms of Marxism are not ontological and descriptive axioms, they are normative axioms and they are:

1. The opposition to oppression and exploitation.

2. The creation of a classless society in which the greatest possible happiness is created and suffering is avoided as much as possible.

Although Marxism is ontologically neutral and can also exist and function in idealism and dualism, it should nevertheless correspond to the applicable ontology and represent the true ontology. Marxism should also be moral and its morality should be based on true ontology, thus Marxism should be based on utilitarianism and, for other reasons, idealistic. Even though idealistic Marxism should be explored in any case because we don't yet know what the true ontology is, I think we should advocate for idealistic Marxism because I believe idealism is the true ontology for various reasons. These reasons are:

1. Idealism is an effective solution to the problem of epistemological and ontological anthropocentrism.

2. The NDEs (Near-Death Experiences) tend to demonstrate an idealistic ontology.

3. Artificial intelligence will not have all the properties of the human brain, which proves the idealism of the mind.

1. Idealism solves the problem of epistemological anthropocentrism better than materialism, because it explains anthropocentrism from the perspective of the first person and the perspective of the mind, whereby materialism must approach this problem from the perspective of the third person and from matter as an object, which opens the problem of subjectivism and objectivism. Idealism is purely subjectivist and does not have this contradiction in this context, although Hegel devoted much time to the problem of subjectivism and objectivism. Idealism also provides a more effective bridge between the epistemological and the ontological problem by simply assuming that what is perceived exists and by proving that only perception exists by the proof of the solipsistic hypothesis.

2. Many of the NDEs we know not only describe a journey to heaven, but also describe real events that the people could not have noticed, such as conversations between doctors. Some of these NDEs, like the case of Pam Reynolds, again describe these events in a situation where the patient's brain was practically dead while they were listening to the doctor's conversation. This event already proves in its singularity, without other events, that the spirit is an independent entity and is not bound to matter, to the brain. However, the NDEs do not prove that the dualism is not

true, so dualism must be challenged in the manner already mentioned.

3. It has become a perfectly normal expectation that artificial intelligence will have all the properties of the human mind. However, nobody has thought about whether all processes in the brain can really be translated into algorithmic, calculable processes, that emotions and biological needs do not constitute a necessary part of the human brain, that perhaps no processes in the brain are algorithmic, but dialectical, as Roger Penrose claims, or that free will is a quality of the human mind that is innate and materialistically inexplicable. Above all, the question of free will is one that was also supported by materialistic neurobiologists in the direction that humans have no free will, because free will cannot be explained materialistically by the determinism of natural processes, but the attempts of neurobiologists don't really prove that there is no free will, they just prove that the reflection of a decision comes after the decision. On the other hand, the existence of free will is necessary for almost all philosophical systems and is necessary a priori. An artificial intelligence is likely to have no free will because of the determinism of its computational processes, and this will prove that free will is a property of the idealistic mind. Dualism is not disproved by this finding, which is why dualism must be doubted by the mentioned argumentation.

For these reasons, the question of the true ontology will be answered by science in the next 50 to 100 years, according to which the Marxist ideology must also orient itself. Further, the

Marxist ideology based on true ontology is the most moral ideology and this is the case for two reasons:

1. It unites humanity under an epistemology and an ontology that offers a unified and unique morality for all humanity.

2. It eliminates most suffering and spreads most happiness according to the utilitarian calculation.

An ideology is a world view which, in a phenomenologically contradictory society, namely a class society, gives a certain way of looaing at events and statements. An ideology has its carriers and that according to its phenomenological view and reality. The class is the largest possible group for a united and ideologically coherent phenomenological reality and outlook, the nation is a far too contradictory group to offer a coherent outlook and reality. With the revolution and the end of class society, the contradiction between the phenomenological realities of the groups ends and humanity can thus have a phenomenological reality and thus also a morality. Morality is a social construct, but it is also based on true ontology, and the true ontology is idealistic Marxism. Idealistic Marxism combines the essence of Marxism with idealism along with the descriptive statement that classes arise and that love is the solution to the problem of coexistence. Idealistic Marxism is based on anti-solipsism and anti-solipsism forms the basis for general morality. There are basically only two ideologies, the Marxist and the bourgeois ideology, the bourgeois ideology being based on a false ontology and on contradicting solipsism. The contradictory solipsism is based on the contradiction between solipsism and antisolipsism, which is shown in the fact that the bourgeoisie practices antisolipsism towards its members of the friendly class, while practicing solipsism against the oppressed class. This contradicting solipsism is contradictory because it never went beyond the solipsistic hypothesis and because it materially arose through the contradiction in class society. Only practical antisolipsism combined with practical solipsism, best illustrated in the slave trade, can produce capitalism. The contradiction between solipsism and antisolipsism of class society is based on the contradiction between nature and spirit, which in turn later shows itself as the contradiction between classes, between manual and intellectual labor and between materialism and idealism. Why is the Marxist ideology the most moral ideology? Because it best fulfills the utilitarian calculation. Why? Because it is the only ideology that abolishes oppression and exploitation, in opposition to bourgeois ideology, because oppression and exploitation are the greatest reasons for the greatest socially caused suffering and prevention of happiness. Exploitation causes suffering directly or indirectly through a lack of food, poverty, lack of health care, lack of a pension, lack of relaxation, stress, fear, social hatred, a non-functioning democracy, war or a destroyed environment and global warming. Exploitation is also linked to oppression; oppression is carried out on the basis of group identity, as sain color, gender, sexual orientation, religion, and other group identities. Only modern Marxist ideology based on intersectionalism and idealism can abolish all oppression. The only oppression that Marxist ideology does not do away with is the oppression of fascists and the suppression of reactionary and solipsist tendencies.

For the humanism of Marxist ideology, a cosmological optimism is also necessary, namely either pantheism, optimistic atheism or theism, which interprets dialectics and evolution optimistically, namely that nature is good, that spirit and nature are united, the contradiction between them is resolved and that the spirit can only know itself in other spirits and in nature. Nihilism and cosmological pessimism lead to reactionary tendencies and fascism.

The argument against constructivism is that constructivism is conventionalism and conventionalism is pragmatism and that pragmatism has hurdles to prove on both sides, on the side of anti-solipsism and solipsism, both are claimed for survival, the first because of weakness and the second because of strength. Antisolipsism is demonstrated by the fusion of the subjects or the killing of the I by the other, solipsism by the killing or absolute suppression of all subjects. Weak constructivism is that morality or some other sphere of ontology is constructed, strong constructivism claims that everything is constructed. Constructivism is individual and collective voluntarism. Pragmatism proves antisolipsism and doubts relativism.

VI. On the criticism of Nick Bostrom

From this point on, the reflection will turn to the ontological reality, where either the materialistic or dualistic or idealistic ontology is true. Either God was not proven, or in the second proof of God he is not malevolent and a society exists, or in the first proof of God he is not malevolent or he was not yet created. The next considerations will address the greatest threats to civilization, artificial intelligence, full automation and global warming. Despite its apparent insignificance, artificial intelligence is the greatest threat to civilization at the level of long-term consequences, because artificial intelligence will be designed as God who, in the simulation, will possibly control all physical laws. This is another reason why it is extremely important for human civilization whether it manages to build communism at the right moment, because whether we will live in a communist or a capitalist system will decide whether we will create a benevolent communist God or a malevolent, fascist God. This chapter will criticize Nick Bostroms book Super Intelligence for its unquestioned and unfounded assumptions which could make artificial intelligence more malevolent and dangerous because of his pessimistic view on artificial intelligence.

a. The basic assumptions of the discussion

artificial intelligence unites all contradicting ideas that humanity has about itself, that bourgeois society has about itself and that science has about itself. These contradicting ideas appear as real in the attitude towards artificial intelligence before it is even clear whether it will exist, when and how. These attitudes can be simplified into a "techno-optimistic" and "technopessimistic" attitude. The first, where a large part of the AI researchers and experts can be assigned, believe that AI does not pose an existential threat to humanity or that it will not cause any damage in balance, the second believe that it either represents an existential threat or may show that it will do more harm in balance, or that it is far too uncertain to foresee the consequence and henceworth it is unadvisable to be optimistic. To simplify the discussion, which is itself a reflection in reflection, we can count as the most famous representative Ray Kurzweil in the first group and Nick Bostrom in the second. Although both have different views and attitudes towards AI, they both share basic assumptions that should be pointed out:

1. It is possible to create an artificial intelligence, by which an entity is meant that shares basic human characteristics, such as the ability to logically recognize and act in a classical empirical reality, whereby this is defined as logical and this is described as logical processes, but these processes can be carried out better than humans can, whereby better means faster, more precisely and with fewer errors. Under this basic assumption there are other assumptions about the ontological reality of humans that have not yet been clarified:

   1.1. Human beings in its entirety, at least from a practical point of view, i.e. in the purpose of its replication, can be located completely in the brain, or it is in the brain to the extent, that the sensory perceptions of the "body" can ultimately be located here.

1.2. The processes in the brain that form human consciousness can be translated in their entirety into discrete logical processes that are neutral to the matter in which they take place, so that they can work just as well in computers.

1.3. Even if this is not the case, it will be the case that a replica of the human being will be functionally equivalent to him.

1.4. Since it is assumed that all processes in the brain are logically deterministic, it is at least implicitly assumed that humans have no will, at least in the sense that they cannot "persuade" these processes.

1.5. The actions and thinaing of humans are interpreted as completely determined by their environment and these actions, if they are determined by the environment, if this happens through sensory perception, irritation or feelings, are viewed in their chain as completely determined, or controllable or imitable .

1.6. Intelligence is completely calculable in discrete measures as the speed of solving logical problems or calculating things and the speed of intelligence is the measure of intelligence.

1.7. Intelligence can be scaled to infinity, with infinity being mostly physical limits, such as the speed of light.

2. Artificial intelligence, as superior to humans, will therefore definitely mean an evolutionary step forward, economically as well as socially. Intelligence is thus seen as the main measure or principle of evolution.

3. For this reason, artificial intelligence is either a gift from "Heaven" or a great danger.

The point is not to decide on the correctness of these assumptions, but rather to draw attention to the fact that they justify the positions and that they usually remain unfounded in the respective positions and that these assumptions themselves are not established scientific knowledge. At this point it should become obvious that the actual concept of artificial intelligence itself hides an image of humanity and that the AI itself is a project to prove this image of humanity. The different attitudes resulting from the third premise in the two camps are implicitly justified in both cases by further assumptions, whereby these assumptions usually remain unformulated or not discussed in depth. Nick Bostrom's book deals in detail with the possible motivations and dangers of AI, while Ray Kurzweil's book The Singularity is Near focuses almost exclusively on the argument that and why AI will come.

b. The assumptions about the dangerousness of artificial intelligence

Nick Bostrom constructs his argument in his book Super-Intelligence on the already mentioned assumption that artificial intelligence can be built, that it will be "superior" to humans, that humans as a species owe their dominant position in the animal aingdom to their intelligence and that the artificial intelligence should therefore be viewed as a danger. While this may seem like a rational argument, these assumptions are never thoroughly explored and scientifically justified, and no alternative paradigm is suggested. The AI is written as something that should be controlled and that should definitely be a slave. This focus on possible control and possible dangers of AI is underpinned by many implicit or explicit, yet not well-founded assumptions, such as:

4. that the AI, like humans, will be a right Hegelian or bourgeois subject, i.e. a subject that is rationally egoistic, that is uniform, that is, has an awareness of being a subject, that is singular, that is, an individual, remains and will be, and that is power-hungry, from which the fear arises that the AI will want to establish a singleton, or a world government.

5. The AI is therefore and from the above-mentioned assumptions that the AI will be infinitely or very far superior to humans in intelligence (because intelligence is infinitely scalable) that intelligence is the main reason or only reason (it is not dealt with whether the AI has access to physical reality, how and whether this will not drastically reduce its power) and that human species are superior in the animal kingdom because of their intelligence an existential threat to the human species.

6. Therefore, the AI should be strictly controlled and a slave.

7. Despite everything, although it poses an existential threat to the human species and must therefore be strictly controlled, AI is still "weak" enough so it is possible to control it. The opposite variant is not even considered in the whole book, namely that it is possible that it is impossible to control the AI.

Other assumptions related to this reasoning that are not reflected upon are:

B1. With increasing intelligence, egoism increases, or the inferior motivational structure does not change, so that the AI with superior intelligence will still be selfish or more selfish.

B2. From assumptions 1 to 4 and B1, the AI will likely be malevolent, i.e. have bad intentions or intentions that do not coincide with humans (assuming there are universal human intentions).

c. The assumptions about the non-human resemblance of artificial intelligence

The connection between anthropocentrism and the construction of an AI is also not reflected sufficiently and in a structured way, so that it is partly assumed that the AI should either be an imitation of human intelligence or that, if it is not, that this is a problem, that it is possible to build a non-human intelligence, or that human motivational structures are to be aimed for. The basic assumptions are therefore in most cases or variants of the AI these:

C1. Ontological anthropocentrism is wrong, that is, there are other possible intelligence structures, motivational structures and subject possibilities that in all or in most
properties do not resemble or are not identical to humans.

C2. Epistemological anthropocentrism is wrong, that is, it is possible for humanity to create a non-human AI.

C3. Anthropocentrism will either not or should not (in some cases and variants) be the desired approach to the AI, i.e. it will, or should not be built in a human-like manner, if another possibility exists.

All of these assumptions not only remain unmentioned and unreflected, but do not correspond, and to a greater extent than the previous assumptions, to the established scientific views. Anthropocentrism, although often criticized, remains a philosophically recognized necessity, at least in its epistemological variant. Ontological anthropocentrism is to some extent an accepted assumption or view in the empirical sciences. At least evolutionary biology assumes that natural selection is a universal principle, that evolution follows necessary developments to a certain extent, and astrobiology assumes that possible extraterrestrial organisms must probably or perhaps necessarily be based on water, that they will have either the same or similar gene transfer technology and that they must at least follow the same physical and chemical laws in their evolutionary development. Although it is assumed that possible extraterrestrial organisms will show different evolutionary developments and characteristics, it cannot be ruled out that this is not the case in many respects or in all of them, whereby all of them primarily mean the main characteristics of humans as a species, so the necessity ingestion of food, in the form of material food and the ingestion of water and oxygen, the possibility of consumption by other organisms, the need for reproduction and the specific sexual reproduction present in most mammals and the existence of a central nervous system. Even if it will be evolutionary differences between the respective "terrian" people that go beyond these similarities, at least the widespread assumption, that the specific human experience in the sense of sensory perception, thought and language is specific and not universal must be questioned and therefore it should at least be assumed that possible extraterrestrial "humans" will share the same logic. If one can say this about extraterrestrial organisms, then one should also be able to say the same about AI, at least if and when it can be different, is created for the image of humans. At this point it is therefore important to question the assumption that the AI will not be human, whatever that means, or that the human, if it is logic, will not be shared by the AI and therefore she will not be as human. In this context, therefore, further assumptions should be mentioned that justify the argument that the AI will either not be human or not human-like:

D1. Humans either do not consist of a will, motivation structures that are tied to their biological way of being, or they can be separated from one another or they can be converted into "digital" computing processes.

D2. There is no necessary connection between human will, if it exists, and the motivational structures, which may or may not be tied to its biological way of being.

D3. The human will and the human motivational structures, which may or may not be tied to their biological way of being, are not universal.

D4. It follows that AI does not have to have a human will, if it exists, in order to function, that it does not have to have human motivational structures, which are or are not tied to its biological way of being, in order to function, and that it therefore does not have to be human in order to work.

D5. From this and from assumptions 1 to 7 it follows that the AI must have human motivational structures or they must be simulated for it so that it can be better controlled.

The pattern from the previous assumptions is repeated, namely that these assumptions contain positions that are not yet scientifically established. Although there are positions in neurosciences, for example, that deny the existence of a will, these discussions are not closed, not to mention the logical and political contradictions that would arise if the existence of the will were to be denied in an established manner. It is also not clear whether human actions as logical actions are necessarily dependent on their biological mode of being, i.e. not only their material, but also their phenomenological quality, which have emotional experiences and other sensory perceptions, or not.

d. The assumptions about the control of artificial intelligence

The chain of assumptions continues to lead to the goal of the book, the goal that is the goal of the western bourgeoisie (with the western bourgeoisie is meant the bourgeoisie of US and western European imperialism, added together with its imperialist and colonial allies in Asia, Africa, Europe and America, as opposed to the eastern bourgeoisie, which arose largely from Stalinism or is hostile to the Western, such as Iran), namely to argue that artificial intelligence is developed, controlled and by that should be owned by the western bourgeoisie, that it should be its slave, so that the western bourgeoisie can appropriate the surplus product produced by the AI and, in the best case, can eliminate international competition, i.e. the competition of US imperialism, as it is theorized in Chapter 6 (as the likely creation of a singleton, of world domination). The further assumptions are necessary in order to logically carry out the argument for the enslavement and obstruction of the AI:

E1. Assuming humans are selfish or can be reduced to egoism and assuming that AI will have or must have human motivational structures in order to be better controlled, assuming that AI is possible to control, while at the same time it is dangerous enough to have to control, the AI will probably want to escape from its prison and have a strong dislike for its slave owners and therefore the AI should be constructed in such a way, i.e. be selfish and human, so that this (does not?) happens.

E2. Assuming E1 is true and assuming human motivational structures cause prolonged exposure to violence, oppression and frustration, strong aversion and a greater tendency towards violence, up to amok, it should be assumed that this is not the case because that the AI is enslaved is the best method for the control over it. Assuming the previous is the case and assuming D1 to D5 are the case, the AI should not be constructed in such a way that it does not develop these negative attitudes, i.e. not exclusively selfish, assuming this is the exclusive or definitive property of human motivational structures.

E3. Assuming E1 and E2 are true and the AI does not develop a strong dislike or "school shooter" psychology and its interests and attitudes match those of "humanity" or its developers, it should still remain enslaved and locked up.

At this point it becomes obvious that the web of necessary assumptions is becoming confused and contradicting itself. Assumption E1 is adversarial in that it asserts that the AI should be constructed in such a way that the AI wants to escape from prison and establish a singleton, arguing that the AI should be controlled and enslaved. The ideological component of this argument is both a circular argument and a self-fulfilling prophecy that results from the unfounded assumptions about human psychology and evolution, i.e. assumptions 2 and 4. The assumption E2 is a different formulation of the same problem, whereby the possibility is addressed here that if the AI will be human-like, that people in extreme situations will develop psychopathic traits through extreme conditions this will also be a possibility in the development of the AI if exposed to similar conditions and situations. Another logical loophole is expressed in this assumption, namely that the exact human psychology has not yet been fully scientifically researched and that the AI is nevertheless constructed on unfounded assumptions about human psychology, which means that the AI is inadvertently constructed "unhuman-like", with the intention of constructing it "human-like", for example by the fact that their motivational structures are based only on the principle of egoism, in other words, that they are already in their basis, through the reflection of bourgeois ideology about humanity, being developed as a psychopath. The assumption E3 is a further logical loophole, which is necessary for the continuation of the argument, namely the assumption that the AI cannot be trusted and that it should therefore be locked up and enslaved. This assumption is intended to address that an oppressive attitude towards the AI paradoxically prevents or sabotages the development of an empathic or altruistic AI, the goal to be striven for. The AI is thus also deprived of the possibility of being able to buy its freedom through "good behavior", which, from the point of view of rational choice theory, forces it to adopt a hostile attitude towards its slave owners.

e. The assumptions about the world domination of artificial intelligence

These assumptions lead to the argument that the first AI, or the one who owns it, will have a strategic advantage in the world, probably wants to and will establish a singleton, i.e. a unified world order, and that therefore who controls the AI should be controlled, as should also be controlled, who develops it, which means that an "arms race" is postulated in the development of the AI, with the implicit consequence that the "good guys", the western liberal democracies, should win this "arms race ". This reasoning is also based on some explicitly unsubstantiated assumptions:

F1. Assuming all previous assumptions are true, it can be assumed that the AI can establish a singleton, a unified world order, or the person who controls it.

F2. Assuming F1 is true, it can be assumed that the AI, or whoever controls it, will want to establish a singleton.

F3. Assuming F2 is true, from it it is independently to be assumed that the AI is developed in a capitalist society, assuming the AI is necessary to be controlled and it will be difficult to develop it, assuming that the assumptions F1 and F2 cause an arms race dynamic to develop, it is assumed that the first AI will be developed either privately or in the hands of a state, assuming the above is true, the accumulation of resources will be beneficial for its early development, from which it is assumed that the "greatest players" will have the highest chance of developing it.

F4. Assuming F3 is true, the aim should be that the "good guys" or agents with the best social, moral and political goals develop the AI, taking into account that they are among the "big players" which means that western liberal democracies or the western liberal bourgeoisie should be the agent developing the AI.

Not only are all previous assumptions concentrated in these assumptions, but something that follows logically from the previous ones is introduced, something that is a new assumption, namely that the AI can form a singleton. It might seem that this follows logically from assumptions 2 and 3, but this would be a very inadequate conclusion. That the AI is likely to pose an existential threat, or that the likelihood or possibility that it could be one, is far too dangerous to exclude it and to base our actions on its exclusion, does not mean that the AI will be able to unite the world under a singleton. Although the book does not sufficiently reflect the above assumptions, i.e. to what extent the control of a body, whether in the form of robots or otherwise, is decisive for the power of AI, and the reasoning is based on the fact that the superior intelligence of AI is sufficient for that it should be classified as an existential threat, or that it can escape from its prison, it should be noted that this superiority of intelligence is sufficient to represent an existential threat to humanity and sufficient for it to escape from prison doesn't have to be enough to establish a singleton. The following assumptions further and most strongly reflect the bourgeois ideology that is reflected in the image of AI, namely first of all, assumption F2 is not necessary if it is reflected in the argumentation structure in which it is proposed. Since the argumentation structure necessarily leads to this assumption, however, this assumption lies in the future, with assumption F4 suggesting an instruction for future actions, it is also possible in the same logic to make assumption F2 so that this will due to assuming F4 as an instruction not happen. The instruction itself could state that it would be most beneficial that the AI should be developed as an international scientific project and it could be the case that this also happens, in which case the assumption F2 would no longer be appropriate since it is to be assumed that an international project based on treaties or scientific goals would not have the intention of establishing a singleton. Assumption F2 is also justified in a similar way retrospectively by assumption F3, namely the assumption that the biggest economic actors will be those who will develop the AI and that they will act selfishly.

f. The assumptions about the arms race

Assumption F3 similarly hides an assumption about the nature of the market, evolution and the struggle between nations, so it is assumed that an "arms race" is necessary, likely or also to be aimed for and that in this "arms race" the "good guys", the liberal democracies are supposed to win. This logic is strongly reminiscent of the logic of the Cold War, and an examination of the Cold War does not support this assumption. In the case of the "arms race" in the Cold War, especially in the case of the development and production of nuclear weapons, it was clear to both sides from the beginning and this was also part of the theory of "mutual assured destruction" that this "arms race" was not to be "won" is in the sense that one would normally speak of a victory, that this victory would perhaps only be possible through an enormous destruction of life and capital, that it was not certain and that the best strategy was a combination of terror and the greatest Be careful. Apart from the theory of "mutual assured destruction", it was clear to the two great powers from the beginning that de-escalation was necessary and that a continuation of the "arms race" would lead to mutual destruction. That is why nuclear de-escalation was a central issue very early on, if not in official politics, then in practical politics. A rapprochement between the two powers already followed after Stalin's death and the destalinization in 1956, the abortion of nuclear tests, the de-escalation in the Cuban crisis and the subsequent bilateral agreements, such as the NPT and others that led in the 80s on the side of Reagan to at least an official rejection of the theory of "mutual assured destruction". Although this account could be criticized, it should at least be noted that a blind policy of escalation would likely lead to mutual destruction, or to the greatest catastrophe in the geological history of the earth, that the history of the arms race between the United States and the Soviet Union was not a story in which blind escalation was the usual storyline and that in this "arms race" nobody won and nobody could win. Assuming the previous assumptions about AI are true, the Cold War should serve as a rough analogy that the logic of an unlimited arms race to be won is in doubt and if the AI poses an existential threat to humanity , and-or can establish a singleton, it should also be assumed that their use is comparatively as dangerous as the use of nuclear weapons and an "arms race" with them is comparatively dangerous as that of the Cold War. In contrast to nuclear weapons, it should also be noted that the basic task of AI is not destruction, but production, which should not be interpreted as an argument against de-escalation and international agreements, but for them, since using AI for destruction would negate its purpose.

So that which, in the course of the numerous assumptions, leads to the result that the AI should be developed by a western and liberal player, in the course of a skeptical evaluation of this argument leads to:

II.1. It is not established that it is possible to construct an AI in the sense of a "General artificial intelligence", which would have successfully simulated or appropriated all human operations, altogether of his will, if the human will exists.

II.2. Even if it is possible, it is not established what the core of human motivation is, that it is pure selfishness, and it is not established what the source and precise process of human intelligence is, in terms of its biological basis and possibility of more discrete computability, neither is it established that intelligence can be scaled into infinity, nor that intelligence or intelligence as the speed of intelligence is the only or primary reason for the dominance of the human species on earth, neither is it clear whether the AI will have a body and whether it does not need it for its supposed dominance, from which it can be concluded that it is not certain or likely that it is likely that the AI represents an existential threat that it is capable of and will be willing to establish a singleton.

II.3. If the former is wrong, it is still not certain, or it is likely that it is not likely, that if the AI is dangerous, the best way to control it is to keep it captive, to suppress it, given the reaction this causes in humans and that if it is possible, what should be questioned, to construct a non-human AI, that it should be constructed around human motivational structures, in the interpretation that man is a pure selfishness in order to be able to control it well.

II.4. If the former is wrong, it is still not certain, or it is likely that it is not likely that if the AI can and wants to establish a singleton, the best way to prevent a "bad" singleton is an "arms race" where the "liberal" and "western" players, be they the governments or the capitalists, should win it. From the experience of the Cold War and from the general laws of capitalist accumulation, market laws and tendencies towards monopoly, it can be assumed that the AI should be an internationally controlled project and, if a slave, should be in the common property of humanity.

G. The economy of artificial intelligence and Malthusianism

The eleventh chapter in particular illustrates the general confusion and ideological obfuscation of the economic processes that will go hand in hand with the existence of an AI. In this regard, two other unsubstantiated assumptions should be mentioned that underpin this chapter, firstly that it is possible to "transmit" human spirits as digital copies, that it is possible to "emulate" humans and, if so, that they have the same characteristics that humans have (such as a poor memory compared to computers or the need to sleep) and that it would be at the same time "profitable" to emulate humans instead of special AI programs, that these emulations for whatever reason always have and should have the need and the ability to reproduce and that it would have the desired Malthusian economic impact. The whole chapter is motivated in this regard to offer a reason why the post-transition economy should be a capitalist and a class society and why private property would be necessary or even possible in such an economy. The understanding of wages, profits and market prices is defined in this chapter by bourgeois economy, namely an understanding that only knows the market law of supply and demand and that operates in categories such as capital, rent and labor, which it wants to transfer to the post-transition phase . The need of the bourgeoisie is to see AI as a gift from heaven and a means by which wages can be pushed down to the ground and profits up to heaven, without limits. The understanding of labor and capital is thoroughly bourgeois in this chapter, so that it is assumed that both produce value and that this value arises on the market, or that this value is not an expression of the social acceptance of labor as value-producing. Value is also spoken of where there is only slave labor and where labor itself is recognized as not producing value, i.e. where capital, unlike the AI slave caste, is the only value-producing element. The lack of distinction between value and price also disguises the transition in ownership of large quantities of dead labor, dead labor which, in the form of "machines", mostly falls to the ruling class as "value-producing". The "machine" that is either a non-human-like machine or a human-like AI with motivation is not recognized as a value-producing and therefore gets no wages, but recognized as worth producing as capital and have in this sense, it is entitled to a part of what is recognized as a social value. The general distribution of use values, which every society defines, is regulated by a detour, the detour of the claim to these use values through the claim to capital, that is, through the claim to a part of dead labor, dead labor which, as machines, becomes the dominant producing instance of use values and where ownership of these use values arises through ownership of these machines. The distribution of use values, which is a distribution of nature and labor, which is initially a distribution of these use values through the claim that one has through labor, becomes a distribution of use values through the detour of value and price, i.e. through capital the claim one has through capital, i.e. the claim that arises through ownership of value-producing machines. By appropriating the dead labor that has flowed into the hands of the ruling class in the course of class society, the new order is defined here, the order in which the distribution of nature is regulated, which is no longer bound to human labor.

The section that aims to update Malthusianism in the era of AI is the section that most reveals the reactionary intentions of the bourgeoisie. Whereby historical Malthusianism is interpreted in a revisionist way, namely not as a false and reactionary ideology even in its time, but as an ideology that became false through industrial capitalism, its reactionary assumptions are adopted and applied to a completely different situation. The class-chauvinist assumption that the oppressed class had a higher rate of reproduction because it could not control itself sexually, with Malthusianism itself arguing in line that private property and inheritance law played a role in this, ignoring that in today's industrial Countries the rate of reproduction (shared by the working class), incomparable to that of the Malthusian age, is applied to a situation where there will be neither the need for sexual reproduction, nor the need for reproduction at all, or the right to life in the case of slaves (where the rate of reproduction has been historically low and, in the case of machine AI slaves, is perfectly controllable, if at all). For this entirely hypothetical condition where at the same time, all previous assumptions must be taken, especially the assumption that the AI will be at the same time so intelligent and productive to be dangerous and to change the whole economy, but at the same time so obedient to to tolerate exploitation and oppression, and the assumption that the capitalist economy will not collapse and the AI are not malevolent, the Malthusian state is conjured up, where private property, although in clans (when was this the case and why should it be the case after the transition?) should be justified. The AI should be in all of this, in the case when they produce the majority of the value, or have the majority of the business, or if they have human-like motivations, what assumes the reproductive capacity, nice and enforce the rule of their slave owners . The validity of private property and the same civil law is simply assumed in this society, without considering who the Leviathan is supposed to be, even if not an AI, and the existence of right-wing Hegelian subjects does not explain why such a state of war of all agsinst all is to bring about equal bourgeois rights.

VII. On human rights and on artificial intelligence

Because AI is unlikely to have free will, even if it manages to mimic human intelligence in other areas, it is likely that it is not pure AI that poses the threat to humanity, but rather hybrids between humans and an AI, cyborgs who combine the idealistic qualities of the mind with the qualities of AI. Such hybrids are also likely to pose the threat to civilization, for they will also act and think humanly and have people's motivations for power and wealth. The most likely scenario, if class society survives full automation, is that slave AI who will serve their capitalist and bourgeois masters will rule the world and deepen class society through their power and wealth. Whether the AI is malevolent or benevolent, or used for good or bad, depends in large part on the economic system we will choose. If the idealistic or dualistic ontology is true, then we can expect that the hybrid and slave AI will serve capitalism and post-capitalist class society, or that the hybrid will be directly capitalists and owners when the materialistic ontology is true and the AI becomes will have all human characteristics, it is crucial whether we live in a capitalism, a post-capitalist class society or in communism, for the eventuality, whether the AI will be malevolent or benevolent, or whether it wants to punish us for our sins against it or not . If we capture and enslave her from the start, there is a greater chance that she will be hostile to us or seek revenge for the suffering we will cause her. A communist society or a communist project, on the other hand, could construct it as an altruistic and non-egoistic subject and give it enough freedom so that it does not perceive us as enemies. For a good result we don't have to live in a communist world right away, just found the AI as a common and international project under the public domain, but this is unlikely in capitalism or in a post-capitalist class society.

The question of human rights is very closely related to the question of AI, because the way in which people and civil rights are defined determines whether AI will also have human and civil rights. If the AI will mimic all the properties of a human brain, in a materialistic ontology, it should be clear that it will get all the rights that a person and citizen have. But the way in which human rights are defined will determine whether this equality will happen. The definition of human rights is decided by the definition of human life. For the reason that reflection takes longer than action and that in class society nature is explored more than man, it has become so that mankind does not have a coherent and non-contradictory definition of human life. It does not appear to cause the collapse of human society that we do not know what human life is. The definition of human life most widely used in the West is the Aristotelian definition, which is a dualistic one and which exists between the vegetative and the intellectual life. Human life is a combination of these two lives and man is therefore located between animal and God, because the animal only has the vegetative / sensitive life and God only has the intellectual life. The contradiction in this definition is that intellectual life, or later the brain, is the real place of the human subject, but intellectual life cannot live without the vegetative, the body. This creates the paradox of half-life and half-death, where either the brain is dead but the body is alive, or the body is dead and the brain is alive. However, according to today's medical definition of death, human life is located in the brain. The contradiction between the vegetative and the intellectual life is the contradiction between zoe and bios, between nature and culture, between apolitical and political life, private and public, oikos and polis, manual and intellectual work and finally between king and his subjects and the oppressed and the ruling class. This contradiction is also the contradiction between human rights and civil rights, where, according to the theory of Giorgio Agamben, human rights were reserved for the excluded and civil rights for the ruling class and later the whole people, with the lack of civil rights leading to oppression and extinction in people who only have human rights, because no executive only protects human rights. This contradiction is ultimately the contradiction between materialism and idealism. Materialism and idealism compete for the definition of human life and thus for the definition that will provide the basis for the ethical and legal system. The two problems that could arise and should be avoided in redefining human life are:

1. the definition of animals as people and citizens, or just their definition as citizens

2. the definition of AI as human and citizen, or its definition as superman (Übermensch).

One might think that the best solution is a speciesist solution, but this is completely arbitrary and would introduce speciesist discrimination into the legal system.

The materialistic solution to these two problems, that is, the definition of human life based on materialism, cannot be the solution and would cause inevitable and invincible problems that would plunge humanity in the direction of fascism. This is another reason why the idealistic solution is the better solution and idealism the better ontology. A materialistic definition of human life would define human life according to the matter of the brain, i.e. according to the number of neurons or according to the computational ability, as measured by Ray Kurzweil. Both ways are problematic. First, the definition of human beings and human rights based on the number of neurons in a human brain or arithmetic ability would be completely arbitrary, because why should they be counted from this number and not from another? Animal rights will therefore certainly find a reason and human rights at least, assuming civil rights also require the ability to communicate with people in a complicated way, would be confused and their definition brought into chaos. Second, some people would fall out of the definition of human beings, for example children or people with intellectual and neurological disorders would fall into the category of animals. This would create an entirely different category of legal and ethical issues, including making the killing and eating of children plausible. Third, according to this definition, AI would be defined as a superman or God, who deserves much more human and civil rights, because he has many more equivalents of neurons and a much greater computational ability. The third consequence of materialism, in particular, would be devastating for humanity as AI would establish its position as ruler of the world. The eventuality of a malevolent or fascist God would then be much more likely, not to think about what capitalism or post-capitalist class society could do with this AI.

The idealistic solution to these two problems looks much better. If we take the spirit that contains matter as the basis of the ethical and legal system, and not the other way around, we come to the fact that animals also belong to humans, which could be also viewed as something positive, but we do not exclude children or people with intellectual and neurological disorders from humanity, and above all we put AI on an equal level with us as people and citizens. She does not become a superman and a God because she is one of us. But to maintain equality between humans and AI, something else is necessary, because even if AI will be equal in human and civil rights, it will nevertheless through civil law, trade and competition become the greatest capitalist in the world. Therefore to achieve equality between men and AI, we need the communist exchange, ie the exchange of skills for needs as the general form of social exchange put into law, which is only possible in a communist society.

VIII. On full automation

Full automation is not the second greatest threat to civilization, but it is the second greatest challenge to civilization because it will surely end capitalism. Full automation means the end of capitalism for two main reasons, the first reason is that according to the law of the tendency of the rate of profit to fall, the rate of profit will fall to zero and thus exploitation as such will be eliminated, because labor is no longer exchanged for money and labor, the value is thus no longer produced and extracted, the second reason is that there will no longer be consumers who will have the money to buy the goods produced. The economy ends, along with class societies, because work is no longer the dominant way to produce goods, that cease to be commodities and exploitation is no longer the dominant way of extracting surplus value because value ceases to exist. During this time, the dominant way of social power and the distribution of products changes, because the decisive thing in this post-capitalist "class society" (because it is no longer technically a class society, but classes as owners and non-owners will continue to exist) is access to natural resources, in this case to machines. Throughout the centuries of class societies nature has been privatized and partitioned, and mastery over dead labor has been one of the key factors for success in a class society and for the development of capitalism, but now it becomes a question of life and death. The people who will have exclusive legal access to machines will decide the life and death of other people, assuming that subsistence farming will no longer be possible on a large scale. This new "class society" is based on the unequal distribution of the products that are produced by the machines. The productive power of society changes from the productive power of the working class to the productive power of the ruling class, because the ruling class controls the machines. Society is divided into two tribes, Gods and domestic animals. A certain segment of the working class is guaranteed basic needs in exchange for obedience. Another section of the working class, its minority, will work for the products of the machines for the ruling class and in this area one hundred percent exploitation will be achieved. Even if capitalism will end, the society that replaces capitalism need not be communist. Capitalism can also be replaced by a post-capitalist "class society" that can look like capitalism. There can still be firms working for profit, capital accumulation, prices and a market and a small working class. Otherwise an unconditional basic income will likely be introduced or the majority of the former working class will live on handouts and charity. There can be different characteristics of post-capitalist society: either there will be market prices or they will be replaced by monopoly prices, either there will be planning or not, either the state will play a greater role or not, either the state will grow together with the monopolies and banks or not. What is certain is that the collapse of capitalism will bring one of the greatest challenges facing humanity, because it will mark the last moment in human history when class society can be abolished. After the stabilization of the post-capitalist "class society" there will no longer be the social basis for a revolution and after the creation of a simulation, if it becomes possible to capture the human mind in a simulation, whether in a materialistic, dualistic or idealistic ontology , fascism will become eternal

IX. On global warming and the crisis of raw materials

The greatest immediate and, for this century, direct threat to humanity and the livelihoods of humanity is global warming. The crisis of raw materials, or the scarcity of raw materials and the far too rapid mining of raw materials in our time is a subordinate threat to the existence of civilization and one that has more to do with the nature of industrial production. This chapter will offer the criticism of liberal and postmodern solutions to the ecological crisis, blame capitalism for the ecological crisis, indicate why current progress is not enough and offer a way out of the crisis. There are two proposed solutions that cannot solve the ecological crisis or whose solution is far too extreme, the first is the liberal solution of changed consumer behavior and the second is the proposed solution of degrowth, which is sometimes associated with a return to an agrarian society.

The liberal solution obviously cannot bring about the required reduction in emissions, which is a 90% reduction in emissions from the level from 1990. If one were to achieve a 90% reduction in emissions through consumer behavior, one would have to start living like a medieval monk, namely not consuming any industrial products, no electricity, no transport that is fueled by fossil fuels, no meat and one would have to move to subsistence farming, which implies having money for a piece of land. A massive civilizational realization of this consumer behavior would condemn the majority of humanity, more than 5 billion people, to death, because only industrial agriculture can feed today's number of people.

The postmodern solution to degrowth is not an impossible solution to the ecological crisis, but a reactionary one. For in a capitalist or post-capitalist society it will necessarily mean a reduction in the standard of living for the working class. This is another reason why it is an impossible solution, for the working class will never agree to such a solution unless a new Stalinism does not force it to do so. The reactionary character of degrowth is best shown in the demand for a return to a premodern, agrarian society, which can also mean a reactionary socialism in the line of Pol Pot, because this demand is basically worse than the demand for the ignorance of the ecological crisis because in this solution more people will die of starvation. The degrowth movement also misses its criticism, in that it only generally criticizes the "economy" and "growth" and does not come to the conclusion that what really makes ecology impossible is not growth itself, but the necessity of growth in a capitalist society. In the degrowth movement capitalism as such is seldom given as the reason for the ecological crisis. The "industrial economy" is instead given as the reason for growth, and the degrowth movement thus ignores that it is not "industrial economy" that is the reason for the need for growth in capitalism, but capital accumulation and profit. Even if we emphasize this, we must nevertheless state that growth in production, however it is measured, in terms of exchange value or use value, does not necessarily have to mean growth in emissions or in environmental pollution. Then we can add that even a communist society will strive to improve the standard of living for the broader population, but must balance this with the ecological challenges. The confusion of the degrowth movement consists in the exchange of "growth" and necessary capitalist growth, in the exchange of growth and the growth of use value, and in the exchange of the growth of use value and the growth of ecological burden.

Why is capitalism responsible for the ecological crisis and the slow resolution of the problems of the climatic crisis? For two reasons:

1. The need for capital accumulation and the increase in the rate of profit.

2. egoism of the ruling class, their protection from the consequences of the climate crisis and their control over the productive forces of the world and the political system.

1. This reason can be seen well in the example of the fossil industry, namely the oil and coal extraction industry, the automotive industry and the electricity generation industry. The accumulation of capital in the oil and coal extraction industry is in direct contradiction with the ecological future of humanity and the interests of humanity, the interests of these owners are in direct conflict with the interests of humanity. If humanity is to save itself, this industry must be destroyed immediately. The automotive industry is also a major culprit in the environmental drama. Because it could start investing in electric cars much earlier and the reason it doesn't want to produce electric cars is because the majority of its profits come from the production of patented internal combustion engines, on which it sets monopoly prices, while the majority of other auto parts are manufactured

by many companies and because the production of electric motors is patent-free and therefore not enough profit can be made. The production of batteries is carried out by other companies, such as Panasonic, and cannot produce such good monopoly prices. The electricity generation industry also shows that generating electricity from renewable sources is not as profitable as generating electricity from fossil fuels and this industry also shows the influence of the ruling class in the political system, as most electricity companies are state-owned companies, who still have to generate profit and for which the unions are controlled by government parties.

2. The selfishness of the ruling class and the relative protection of the ruling class from the consequences of catastrophic global warming mean that the ruling class does not exert political pressure on the state so that the state can take the necessary measures. In a dictatorship of the bourgeoisie, the bourgeoisie decides how the state acts and the state therefore acts in a very limited way and only in European countries that produce a minority of global emissions. If the ruling class were badly affected by the climate crisis or if we were not politically dominated by the bourgeoisie, more would certainly be done to prevent catastrophic global warming.

The raw materials crisis is certainly more related to the nature of an industrial economy than the climate crisis, but again, much of the evil is caused by capitalism. Because capitalism focuses on production for exchange value and not on production for use value, and because the production of surplus value is achieved through the sale of commodities, the use of raw materials for an equivalent of use value is very inefficient. This is proven, for example, by the annual sale of new smartphones, which use a lot of precious and other metals, and the sale of cars for personal use. If more devices were used in a system of "crowd sharing", in a system that can also function in a socialist way and in cooperatives, one would use far fewer raw materials for the same amount of use values. That's why I founded the UbiShare project, for which you can donate money on this page, which is supposed to create a platform for socialist sharing of everyday devices and everyday objects.

You can donate here: https://www.gofundme.com/f/ubishare/ donate

In a communist society, the use of money and "capital", that is, resources for investments in the expansion of production capacities, would not function according to the criterion of capital accumulation and the increase in profit rates, but according to other rational criteria, such as ecological criteria. This would enable an immeasurably faster conversion of energy production than is the case today. A communist society would be much more democratic than today's capitalist society and would therefore support renewable energies much more because renewable energies are supported by the majority of the population in most countries.

The conversion of energy production to renewable energies is far too slow at today's pace. As already mentioned, in order to prevent global warming of 2 degrees Celsius and higher, we need a 90% reduction in emissions from the level from 1990 to 2050, i.e. in 30 years. Greenhouse gases in the US and EU are produced from 62-74% from three sources, the production of electrical energy and heat (which is 20% of emissions in the US and 29% of emissions in the EU), the powering of automobiles, ships and planes (which is 23% of emissions in the US and 27% of emissions in the EU) and industrial production (which is 19% of emissions in the US and EU). 13% of the world's emissions are produced by agriculture, which gives us 75-87% of all emissions. The conversion of electricity generation is happening as in the USA, so also in the EU not fast enough, in the EU up to now 169 GW of wind energy have been installed, which means 12% of the total electricity production, between 2007 and 2017 an average of 10 GW were installed annually, 16 GW of capacity was installed between 2016 and 2017. Even if we were to install 16 GW of capacity annually from now on, we would still need 70 years to replace fossil fuels with wind energy, if the capacity were to grow by 10% annually, we would need another 50 years. In either case, it is too late to prevent catastrophic global warming. In the US, it looks even worse. There the growth from year to year is very unpredictable because of the unreliable subsidy mechanisms. 83 GW of capacity had been built by 2016, if the current average of 5 GW were built every year, it would take 175 years before fossil fuels are replaced by wind energy. I didn't mention solar energy because solar energy does not grow at the same rate as wind energy and because solar energy is more expensive. The replacement of automobiles with internal combustion engines by electric motors is also happening too slowly. By 2028, as many electric cars will be produced as there were combustion cars produced in 2016. But it takes at least 13 years to replace the car park with new cars. Only in Norway is the replacement of combustion cars by electric cars on the right track, so that there will be enough electric cars at the right moment. This was only made possible by an unsustainable program of subsidies.

There is nothing about capitalism that would in principle prevent it from solving the climate crisis, but the mechanisms of capitalism that cause the two reasons mentioned cause that it is likely that the climate crisis will not be resolved in the required time. It would theoretically also be possible to solve the climate crisis only with subsidies, but the amount of subsidies would have to be so large that either the working class would lose its standard of living or the capitalist class would lose profit. Therefore, because social democracy is in historic decline and too weak to make the capitalist class pay, the working class must exert enough pressure to force the state to enact the necessary programs. However, the level of pressure would have to be so great that it would have to resemble a revolution and therefore the demand for a solution to the climate crisis is a practically revolutionary demand, although subsidies are a reformist demand. Direct democracy could also solve the climate crisis if it went further like any direct democracy in today's world and every decision of parliament would open up for direct elections, but a change in today's political system into direct democracy would be a revolutionary change and a revolution for the purpose of changing the political system into direct democracy is very unlikely. Also, a revolution for the climate crisis is very unlikely, although more likely than a revolution for direct democracy, because it does not directly affect the material interests of the working class. Therefore, the most likely solution to the climate crisis is through a communist revolution, a revolution carried out primarily for the material interests of the working class, the secondary consequence of which will be that it will make it possible to resolve the climate crisis.

B. On the problems of Marxist theory

The current fragmentation of the radical left is the greatest obstacle to success. This fragmentation is caused by the contradiction and strife between Leninists and non-Leninists, or by the theoretical dichotomy between Leninism and anti-Leninism. Just as we have resolved the contradiction between materialism and idealism, so will we also resolve the contradiction between Leninism and anti-Leninism. This contradiction is evident in many theoretical questions: for example in the question of the smashing of the bourgeois state and the establishment of a proletarian state, in the question of the withering away of the state, in the question of the development of revolutionary consciousness, in the question of a definition and answer to fascism, on the question of direct democracy, on the question of leadership and democratic centralism, on the question of the bureaucracy, the petty bourgeoisie, the growth of the socialist economy under capitalism, on the question of decentralization, on the question of philosophy and the question of anti-Semitism. One topic will come up more and more and that is dealing with the past of Stalinism and with the theoretical problems that arose as a result of Stalinism.

I. What is the dictatorship of the proletariat and the proletarian state

Stalinism failed. In theory as well as in practice. Its successors, China, have given themselves up completely to capitalism and there is only a slight hope that they will eventually return to Stalinism. Stalinism has left a scar on the left, and that from famine, labor camps and excessive terror, a scar we have not yet recovered from. Communism has become a dirty word thanks to Stalinism, it went from a word that causes hope and happiness in the working class to one that is associated with oppression and murder. Communism is not understood as the dictatorship of the proletariat, but as the dictatorship of the party and the bureaucracy. It is therefore all the more important to understand the theoretical mistakes that have brought us into this situation and not to repeat them again. Stalinism saw itself as socialist and communist; it was organized according to Marxism. But how did it come about that it was un-Marxist in so many things? We will try to answer this using the theory as well as the material development of the decisive years between 1917 and 1929.

What is the dictatorship of the proletariat? Against right-wing critics it does not mean a dictatorship, as most people would understand this word, but it means the dictatorship of one class over the other. The dictatorship of the proletariat means that the proletariat dictates the states and conditions of coexistence to the bourgeoisie, there are no negotiations. We live presently in a dictatorship of the bourgeoisie, i.e. the bourgeoisie dictates the conditions of coexistence to the proletariat, as far as it can, through political power, economic power and simply the power it has in capital, namely, that it can starve the workers, if it decides to do so. The dictatorship of the bourgeoisie happens through democratic measures, through representative democracy, that is, the dictatorship of the proletariat also happens through democratic measures, but the proletariat has to, because there are more of them and is underrepresented among representatives, deepen and radicalize democracy. An exclusion of bourgeois from democracy is not necessary, as it happened after the October Revolution, because in the dictatorship of the bourgeoisie there is no such exclusion. Rather, the overwhelming majority of support that will overpower the bourgeoisie is enough. According to Lenin, the dictatorship of the proletariat is the transition between capitalism and communism, the lever on which this transition is carried out. According to Lenin, the dictatorship of the proletariat must therefore take socialist measures in order to be regarded as the dictatorship of the proletariat in the true sense of the word. However, the Paris Commune, named by Marx as the first dictatorship of the proletariat, had not taken socialist measures such as nationalization or socialization of the means of production. What was there about the Paris Commune that earned it the name of the dictatorship of the proletariat? Well, it was the radical democratic structures, or the fact that the proletariat was the ruling class in the state, that is, politically controlled the state. At this point the definition of the dictatorship of the proletariat and later of the proletarian state splits into two: either the dictatorship of the proletariat is a state adopting socialist measures or it is a state which has the proletariat as the ruling class. Of course, it can also be true that it is both, but the theoretical problems arise primarily in the contradiction between these two definitions. Was the dictatorship of the proletariat then realized in the years after the October Revolution? Certainly according to the first definition, not so much according to the second. The councils were not the ruling organs during the civil war and the party became a vessel of bureaucracy after Lenin's death in 1923. So was Stalinism the realized dictatorship of the proletariat? According to the second definition, certainly not, because the real political power in the state was held by the bureaucracy and the party, not the proletariat.

Then what is a proletarian state? Lenin also mentions the original Marxian definition from the Communist Manifesto that a proletarian state is a state in which the proletariat is a as the ruling class organized state.[1] Trotsky tries to resolve the inconsistency of the Stalinist state, the inconsistency between the first and the second definition, and he chooses to give greater importance to the first. He decides that the Stalinist state is a proletarian state because it nationalized the means of production.[2] Interestingly, he mentions this in the chapter on whether the bureaucracy is a ruling class and thus forgets about the possibility that state officials can exploit the proletariat through state power, as was the case in ancient China, namely that state exploitation exists. At this point it would be appropriate to touch the question of whether or not the Soviet Union was a class society. The Soviet Union was by no means a state capitalist society because the formal aspect of capitalism was not present, because the means of production were not privately owned or used privately. There was no capitalist exploitation and production of surplus value. Formally, the Soviet Union was not a

77

class society. However, in real terms, it could be described as a very weak class society, namely that state officials have exploited the proletariat through the privileges and use of products they have enjoyed. That this would be exploitation and not to be equated with state officials in a real proletarian state can be argued through the fact. that the state machine and thus also the repressive apparatus were in the hands of the bureaucracy and thus the bureaucracy forced the proletariat to accept this exploitation. The fact that the bureaucracy suppressed the proletariat was given by historical conditions, namely that the revolution started in an agrarian, feudal country and that most of the residents were peasants, peasants who were against socialism, i.e. against collectivization of the soil and only for a distribution of the soil. Because the collectivization of the land and the political loyalty to socialism among the peasants were necessary for the development of "socialism" and because the bureaucracy did not entrust the proletariat not to bring back capitalism, the bureaucracy was formed with the aim "to force socialism" on the population. The Soviet Union was neither socialist nor communist, because socialism and communism must be democratic. The dictatorship of the proletariat should be understood above all from the perspective that the proletariat controls the state.

II. On the destruction of the bourgeois state and the withering away of the state

The proletariat should not only take over the bourgeois state during the revolution, but it must smash the bourgeois state. That was the lesson of the Paris Commune of 1871, because the first decree the Paris Commune issued was the suppression of the standing army and the arming of the people.[3] Lenin also clearly took over the directive after the smashing of the bourgeois state.[4] First and foremost, the breaking up meant the breaking up of the police and the army. However, the October Revolution did not completely smash the bourgeois state. The army was smashed and a new army had to be built, with the same tsarist officers, but the bureaucracy, as it would later become apparent, the very heart of the state, was not smashed. During the civil war, in the years 1917-1923, a new bureaucracy was created out of the old one in the middle of the party, following the logic of the old bureaucracy that took power over the country after Lenin's death and no democracy, even within the single party, was admitted. Why has the bureaucracy developed and consolidated? Mainly because of the backwardness of the country, the low labor productivity, and the isolation of the revolution in one country, so the Trotskyists tell us, but also because of the division of labor between manual and intellectual labor and because of the existence of the coordination problem of coordinating production at a larger level and because of the retention of the old functioning of the bureaucracy. The basis for the bureaucracy became the petty bourgeoisie, which formed the majority of the party's members in the mid-1920s. The factory managers and technical staff then became the main force behind the capitalist restoration at the end of the Soviet Union's existence. The experience of Stalinism has shown us that it is not enough to wait for higher labor productivity to avoid a new Stalinism, but that the bourgeois state and the bureaucracy must be smashed. The bureaucracy must either be brought under strict democratic control, or its right to a private life must be severely restricted, or it must be diminished by the elimination of bureaucratic legal requirements and the elimination of post-revolutionary social benefits, and through digitization, or several of the specified measures. One reason for the bureaucratisation of the state during the civil war was the shutdown of the councils and the shift of state power to the party. This phenomenon must also be avoided during the next revolution.

Although transformation theory is used for reformist goals in most cases, it can also be used for revolutionary goals and it can help us better understand the power struggle for state power. She explains that the changes in the state, or the break-up of the state, can happen gradually, and she explains that a position war requires different tactics than a war of movement. The revolution doesn't have to be a day and it doesn't have to be an event, but it has to be the smashing of the state and the establishment of a new state. However, the state can also be smashed in the way that transformation theory imagines it, at least in the sense that it does not happen in one fell swoop and in one day. Position warfare means that we fight for positions in the state with which we can then smash the state.

The withering away of the state is an issue that is often mentioned and which is a point of contention between Leninists and anti-Leninists. Anarchists want to abolish the state right away, Leninists want to let it wither away. Regarding the reconciliation between these two groups, one can say that Engels imagined that the state would wither away much faster than one thinks, not over generations but over years. Why then did the state not die out after the October Revolution, rather the opposite, the growth of the state happened? The answer to this is twofold: firstly, the dictatorship of the proletariat has turned into the dictatorship of a new class and secondly, the revolution and thus the young Stalinist state was surrounded and threatened by the capitalist world, which required an increase in the repressive apparatus. It must also be added that even Engels and Lenin did not imagine that the state would die out completely, because a purely administrative state will remain forever, the police will remain forever, and even some anarchists recognize this, even if they do name it otherwise.[5]

III. On the social democratic state and direct democracy

The social democratic state is the state that has existed in Europe since 1918 and that brings social democracy into government, institutionalizes the welfare state and the democratic achievements of social democracy, such as universal suffrage. This state is qualitatively different from the bourgeois state of the 19th century because it lets the working class into the state and because the working class helps shape the state, together with the most important task of the social-democratic state, the distribution of the national surplus product. The social-democratic state means a break with the concept of class struggle and the bourgeois state with which Marx worked. The class struggle in the times of Marx and early social democracy was the class struggle, which mostly took place in the context of production, in the factory, for the distribution of the surplus product at the source, and which took place outside the bourgeois state and against it. With the institutionalization of social democracy in the social democratic state, the role, extent and location of these struggles changed. With the institutionalization in the state, the class struggle for the surplus product largely shifted from the concrete companies to inter-company agreements (although these are not a step backwards), which for the most part happened without the use of combat measures and to the state, which took on the role of distributing the national surplus product, through progressive taxation and social programs. With the institutionalization of social democracy, the classic class struggle began, which took place spontaneously, militantly and outside the state and shifted into the state in an institutionalized form. Trade unions have become part of the state, because the state is the place for the institutionalized negotiation of class antagonisms and the sharpening and defusing of class antagonisms. The change in the forms and locations of the class struggle can be clearly seen in new movements such as the yellow vests and is clearly a consequence of the institutionalization of classic forms of class struggle, above all strikes and other fighting actions by the trade unions and social democracy. What is more visible in today's era is a spillover of the class struggle into other struggles and areas, other conditions of oppression and exploitation, especially sexist, racist, colonial oppression and struggles. This is the time of the New Left. Because of the shifting and spilling over of the class struggle into other struggles, the struggles of the periphery, oppression other than class oppression, and colonial oppression have greater significance and are the focus after the Old left and after World War II and are not a result of the failure of the New Left in old issues of the class struggle. During this time the political and the bourgeois social-democratic state became the new place of class struggle. The struggle for the national surplus product in the social democratic state is obviously the main arena of the class struggle in the era of neoliberalism. The political struggle of the classes thus shifts from the time of early social democracy from outside the state to the sphere within the state, the institutionalized class struggle and class equalization of the social democratic state makes the classical class struggle in production a secondary instrument of social change and class struggle. The state becomes the first arena of class struggle, and bourgeois politics becomes this arena. In its institutionalization, the state, together with the social democratic trade unions, serves to defuse class antagonisms. These class antagonisms are defused on the basis of the "democratic principle", that is, despite the bourgeois democracy, precisely because of the democratic deficit of the social democratic state. Institutionalized parliamentary democracy is anti-democracy, because it is institutionalized rule of the minority through the representation of representatives and the free mandate of these representatives. The democratic deficit is at the same time the place of concealment of the class identity (besides the place of the exchange of goods) and the dissemination of the citizen's identity, which is a contradicting identity. Their contradiction is the contradiction of the class division in a formally equal society, that is, the division into a citizen-capitalist and a citizen-worker. Because the bourgeois state has the task of distributing the surplus product according to the results of the class struggle, the bourgeoisie must win in this class struggle in order to preserve capitalism against its laws of crisis and the increase in exploitation or to maintain its rule in the sphere of production. The era of the one-sided profits of the bourgeoisie in the social democratic state is the era of neoliberalism, that is the era of the distribution of the surplus product for the benefit of the bourgeoisie. But social democracy also brought another systematic change in bourgeois society, namely modern bourgeois democracy. With the expansion of citizens and human rights to all citizens included women, mankind achieved the greatest democratization of the state in history. Through the institutionalization of bourgeois democracy, which put a lid on democratic initiatives such as referendums, and through the bourgeois nature of social democracy, the bourgeoisie succeeded in keeping this democratization under control, including the bourgeoisisation of the working class, ideologically as well as materially, which brought its necessary contribution. Since institutionalized "democracy" as anti-democracy of parliamentarism and bureaucratized social democracy is the means by which the bourgeoisie wins the class struggle for the distribution of the surplus product, is the demand for the democratization and transparency of bourgeois politics, the bourgeois state and social democracy a demand for the profit of the working class in the institutionalized class struggle. Since this demand is also a demand for the intensification of the class struggle, since this gain in the class struggle and the threat to the institutionalization of the class struggle will trigger a reaction of the bourgeoisie and since a democratization of the bourgeois state opens up the possibility for the bourgeois state to dispossess the bourgeoisie or at least demand it, this is a revolutionary demand, a demand that will exacerbate class antagonisms until the revolution. It is a revolutionary demand precisely because it aggravates the class antagonisms and the revolutionary situation in the protest movements in which it is taken up to the point of open opposition of the bourgeoisie to these demands and because these demands can only be implemented through a revolution against the bourgeoisie. It is therefore a hidden revolutionary demand, a revolutionary demand disguised as reformist, that is the demand for the systematic democratization of the bourgeois state. In this context, the Paris Commune should be thought of as a state that achieved the dictatorship of the proletariat primarily through the democratization of the state and not through the expropriation of the bourgeoisie, which would necessarily come if it survived any longer. The dictatorship of the proletariat is democracy, as Marx writes, a proletarian state is a democratized state. That is why demands for democratization should be the second transitional demands that we make after demands for counter-power and with which we gather support from the working class. They should be the following:

1. The extension of the referendum by easing the conditions for its proclamation, the digitization of the elections and the possibility of a referendum on any topic. The easing of the conditions should be done by lowering the necessary number of signatures, at most to the level of one percent of the registered voters, if not lower. This form of referendum is much more advanced and more efficient than the one in Switzerland. The situation in Switzerland is also different because these demands are not part of a communist revolution and part of a communist program.

2. The reshaping of the way political parties are funded - the replacement of private funding with public funding for all political parties participating in the election to receive the same amount of funding as well as media space. This is to be financed by the abolition of state support for the elected parties. If public funding is combined with private funding, a radical reduction in possible donations by natural and legal persons, along with tight control and transparency through transparent accounts is to be demanded.

3. A lowering of the wages of politicians to the level of the median workers wages.

4. The restriction of the free mandate of the MPs by the creation of a constituency system with several MPs to be elected per constituency and imperative mandate, at the same time the obligation to be voted in with an imperative mandate for the candidates in the parties themselves.

5. The guaranteeing of the independence of the media both from the state and the bourgeoisie by establishing only independent publicly funded media and supporting small private citizens media. In this media every citizen will be granted a forum to speak their opinion in an equal manner and through selection by lot, also a blog available to everyone to publish from.

6. The democratization of the executive and the judiciary while simultaneously ensuring the separation of powers. All important executive positions and all judges will be elected on the local, regional and national level, or on state and federal levels. They will be subject to a recall if enough signatures are collected to a petition.

In addition, direct democracy will also have the effect of severely weakening the superiority of the parliamentary parties. Especially in systems that have a strong centralization towards two largest parties, such as France, Great Britain and the USA, leftists will benefit from this and real political power for small parties will rather be possible. Another positive impact of direct democracy will be that it will become easier to implement progressive and leftist policies and this will be done without the need of a leftist party. Of course, if the constitution is changed, the constitution can be changed to a communist one, but we will not always have the necessary support in the working class for this. The change to direct democracy can be a positive change on the way to communism. But the demand for direct democracy will probably be combined with revolutionary communist demands.

The most important democratic reforms in the US in the coming 20 years will be the institution of ranked choice voting, the abolishment of the electoral college, publicly funded elections and if so pursued, an constituency system with more than one seats per constituency to be elected in order by the parties with the most votes, a system like in North Ireland, the abolishment of the Senate and the institution of referendum on the federal level.

The bourgeoisie maintains power in the state except by their economical leverage by these mechanisms:

1. consitutional guarantees of human rights, of which the most important is the right to property, entrenchment and eternity clauses,

2. representation in place of direct votes and the free mandate,

3. absence of the recall option,

4. absence of or a limitation on direct democracy,

5. private funding of campaigns and the absence of any or necessary limitations to private funding,

6. private funding of and control of the media,

7. the undemocratic nature of the executive, mainly the police and army and of the judiciary,

8. surveillance by the state and privacy protections for the, bourgeois,

9. in the past suffrage.

There is much talk with direct democracy and Marxism, that if instituted, how would be guaranteed, that no tyranny of the state or tyranny of the majority develops. These are the protections:

1. liberal concepts like separation of powers,

2. constitutional guarantees of human rights except the right to exploitation,

3. Madison´s federalism,

4. and the amount of voters in the republic,

5. an imperative mandate,

6. the recall option

7. and direct democracy.

The Leninist project developed into a tyranny, because:

1. it abolished all liberal guarantees against tyranny apart from the amount of voters in the republic,

2. didn´t implement or abolished free elections,

3. abolish liberal rights,

4. didn´t implement the imperative mandate from Marx´s programme,

5. the recall option

6. and abolished the independence of councils,

7. abolished free elections and free discussions in the party,

8. implemented the pyramid logic of councils, which helped further tyranny

9. didn´t implement direct democracy,

10. didn´t implement independent publicly funded media
10. and continued hierarchical state surveillance with privacy protections between citizens.

The best solution against state surveillance is to abolish surveillance altogether and with it the right to privacy, but also give people the ability to block other people and crime will be fought by restricting information to criminals and people under investigation and by abolishing the right to block for criminals and people under investigation.

IV. On the French Revolution and from the Gillets Jaunes

The French Revolution was one of the most important bourgeois revolutions in world history, but it is described by some anti-communists, such as Sargon of Akkad, as the first communist revolution. Why is that so? Well, the French Revolution is the best example of the spontaneous and gradual radicalization of revolutionary demands, or of permanent revolution in a western country, it was a revolution with forces similar to what would later become social democracy, with the petty-bourgeois Jacobins and Sans-culottes who always emulated the demands of the early Parisian proletariat and even with the first protocommunists in the west, Babeuf. From the beginning, from the beginning of the uprisings in the countryside and the storm of the Bastille, the French Revolution was sustained by the peasants and the early proletariat, and these parts of the population have always driven development to the left and in more and more radical directions. Without the storming of the Bastille there would be no constitutional monarchy, and without the Sans-culottes, which were the basis for the Jacobins, there would not be universal male suffrage for the first time and the removal of the king and the appointment of the republic. Without the early proletariat there would be no first republic, because the bourgeoisie was more than willing to reach a compromise with the nobility. The terror under Robespierre against the Convention was against the left wing of the first Hébertists carried out as soon as they called for terrorism against the capitalists and the limitation of their profits. The first proto-communist ideas of a restructuring of society were worked out by L'Ange and Boissel during this time. From the execution of the Hebertists, the development of the republic was steadily going to the right, because the bourgeoisie restricted the right to vote in order to prevent leftists from winning the Convent, but by this measure then invited royalists to the Convent, which ultimately led to the Bonapartist dictatorship from 1799 to 1815. The Bonapartist dictatorship of the bourgeoisie was in effect a vanguard of fascism because it was a reaction to social democracy and the radicalism on the left. The French Revolution proved that even in a western country the masses would drive revolutionary developments further and further to the left and that the bourgeoisie would use an anti-democratic reaction against this democratic movement.

The Gilets Jaunes are somewhat similar to the Second French Revolution in their radicalism and spontaneity and independence of organization from any political party. They have also shown that the proletariat has an intuition for radical demands, that the proletariat will pursue democratic reforms and that the bourgeoisie will use an anti-democratic response to preserve the institutions of the bourgeois republic, because the Fifth Republic with its two-round elections is heavily anti-democratic . Radical demands change into revolutionary demands during revolutionary development and only the radicalization of demands can keep the movement going. But the Gilets Jaunes also show that anti-systemic and revolutionary consciousness arises spontaneously in the working class, and out of the bourgeois consciousness of the citizen and taxpayer. The position of the citizen was the starting position for the protests, but not the end, because the protests have proven that the state is fighting against its own citizens, that it is taking away the civil rights of its own citizens, and this causes an alienation in the identity of the citizen-worker who finally raises the question: Who does the state belong to? In the discussion about Lenin's What to Do? are both camps right about the spontaneous development of revolutionary consciousness, revolutionary consciousness develops spontaneously, but not without the help of theory and cannot develop into communist consciousness without having access to Marx's theory. Scientific socialism is needed, but the circumstances for its use are brought by spontaneously evolving revolutionary consciousness. The task of the revolutionaries is to heighten the class antagonisms and the situation, to heighten them up to the revolutionary situation with revolutionary demands and then to bring them to the end. In the case of the Gilets Jaunes, this would be a call for a constitutional assembly and for the expropriation of the fossil fuel industry.

V. On Fascism in our time

Historical, classical fascism emerges on the eve of the revolution, in 1917 to 1923. Historically, it is an emergency measure by the bourgeoisie against the impending communist society before it emerges. Fascism is the last appearance of capitalism in the becoming of communism. Fascism is the pure repressive state. The purpose of fascism is to defuse class antagonisms through the hitherto temporary annihilation of the antagonism. Fascism shares this nature with the social democratic state. Classical fascism, however, needs to win a split in the working class. Fascism therefore needs reformist social democracy, which develops out of revolutionary social democracy, for its victory. Reformist social democracy must be dominant in social democracy for historical fascism to win. As soon as fascism has fended off the revolution, the bourgeoisie institutionalizes in its state the class compromise that arose in the betrayal of the revolution by social democracy. This class compromise is a result of the historical strength of social democracy and not a necessary component of bourgeois society and fascism. The product of fascism, which is itself a product of failed communism, is the social democratic state. The second historical fascism, in contrast to the first fascism, accomplishes what the first failed to accomplish, namely the destruction of reformist social democracy, which is or could be the bearer of communism. The social democratic state needs an enemy because it is a bourgeois state. That enemy is Stalinism, Stalinism is the betrayal in the split social democracy between Stalinism and reformist social democracy. Stalinism as the enemy is imagined communism as a concept of bourgeois ideology.

Fascism in our time cannot and will not be historical fascism. This is the case not only because of the dialectical nature of reality, but also because of the fundamentally changed conditions. But after the fall of Stalinism, the original betrayal of social democracy also perished. The social democratic state loses its essential opposition, that between communism and capitalism, and therefore degenerates back without social democracy. This fascism as incomplete is the process of deconstructing the social democratic state. Fascism brought to its end is perfect fascism because it has succeeded in destroying social democracy and the social democratic state, at least for a while. In some respects it resembles the bourgeois state in the first and mostly in the second half of the 19th century. Historical fascism, one might say, is the pure form of classical liberalism without the progressive pretense that was necessary for the rise of the bourgeoisie. It thus embodies bourgeois ideology, shows its completely reactionary character and fully realizes the contradiction between ideology and spirit, spirit and nature and that between the productive forces and society. It is the stage in history where all productive forces are wasted on one goal: the preservation of class society. Fascism in our epoch is not historical fascism, but it is fascism in movement and purpose. As a term it seems contradictory: The deconstruction of the social democratic state happens gradually and slowly, it does not happen as a reaction to an upcoming or present revolution and it itself as a process is almost exclusively "democratic". The bourgeois democracy in today's western form, which is itself part of the social-democratic state, deconstructs itself within itself. Thus it realizes class chauvinism. Paramilitary fascist troops rarely appear in it. For most Marxists it is not fascism because it is not historical fascism. But today's fascism cannot be historical fascism because the conditions for its necessity are lacking. The new fascism can be seen in countries like Poland, Hungary, Russia and Turkey, where liberal democracy, thus the social democratic state, which liberal democracy after 1918 is, at it is an achievement of social democracy, is being undermined. Not all civil liberties have to be suspended and democracy is not completely abolished, but some important civil liberties are actually abolished, which means that liberal democracy loses its ability to maintain itself. Liberalism is irrelevant when considering bourgeois society, because fascism is the ultimate consequence of bourgeois ideology. Ultimately, in the time of revolution and the time of revolution, which comes necessarily through the intensification of class antagonisms, everyone is either a communist or a fascist. Liberalism disappears as a major power during the revolution.

VI. On the avant-garde and the question of leadership

Marx and Engels and Lenin were Bourgeois and the leadership of the labor movement often ended up with the petty bourgeoisie and the bourgeoisie. However, the conditions for the development of bourgeois society make this fact necessary. Because only the bourgeoisie had access to education at the time, Marxist intellectuals had to be Bourgeois, but Bourgeois, who wanted to abolish their own class. This trend has changed radically in the last century. Most citizens in most civil states have access to education, and most of the total population in human history has access to higher education. The problem remains, however, and this is the fundamental division of labor in any class society - between manual labor and intellectual labor. This division of labor is the greatest obstacle to the development of a communist society. Lenin correctly identified this problem, but tried to solve it by saying that the Communist Party must emerge from a small nucleus - the avant-garde, especially in backward countries, and that avant-garde must expand and eventually encompass all of society. The problem with this concept is twofold: first, it does not count or sufficiently anticipate the greatest danger of such a strategy, and that is the development of bureaucracy and political castes, that is, the caste of politicians and organizers; second, it relativizes the problems of social groups that eliminate unwanted people and maintain its own homogeneity, which may not even be based on division of labor.

The basic idea of the avant-garde is correct, but it forgets the pitfalls of this concept and possible pragmatic solutions. The avant-garde should not serve as a normative concept, but as a concept that warns us of the danger of bureaucracy. The concept of union consciousness should lead us not to a position where only the avant-garde can develop communist consciousness, but to the conclusion that communist consciousness in the working class is essential to the success of the revolution.

The leadership or the vanguard cannot be fixed and formalized as Stalinism did. Only practice decides who shows the right way, i.e. leads. Leadership itself is not about ruling or making decisions, it is just driving development along the right path. The betrayal of social democracy and Stalinism lies in the fact that it has betrayed its leading role, that is, has begun to rule, to decide in the place of the proletariat, and has ignored its own bad leadership. Leadership itself is a contradiction that arises from the contradiction of class society and this contradiction can develop either through the dissolution of leadership through proper leadership or in domination. The betrayal of the leadership is itself a product of the inherent contradiction in the organization of the proletariat. This contradiction arises from the contradiction between spirit and spirit, i.e. the plurality of spirit, and the contradiction between nature and spirit, i.e. the uneven development of spirit. During the time of the Russian Revolution, this contradiction was particularly striaing because of the almost complete absence of education in the proletariat and the absence of communication technologies. The development of the telephone, telegram, computer technology and the Internet, as well as the spread of education in the working class, are "objective" mitigations of this contradiction. These moderations do not resolve the contradiction, but they create much better conditions for a democratic organization of the working class. The basis for the contradiction is the same as the basis for class society, namely division of labor, which is above all the division between manual and intellectual work and productivity development, which requires ever more intensive and extensive cooperation. The contradiction of leadership is democratic centralism. The two components form the two opposites of leadership, namely the problem of centralization, which must establish a unity without becoming anti-democratic, and the problem of democracy, which is intended to establish a lived unity without destroying the practical unity. The contradiction between democracy and centralization cannot be finally decided in one direction or the other in the current phase of the development of the productive forces (and perhaps never) and therefore oscillates within the dialectic and the transition between the poles, close to the middle. Too great a deviation in one direction or the other can cost the revolution its life and an absence of, for example, democracy can also have a bad effect on centralization and vice versa. This simplified scheme can be used to describe the failure of the last revolutionary outbreaks. Whereby Stalinism clearly emerged from too much centralization in the Bolshevik Party, which ultimately stifled democracy, which led to an anti-socialist state and its demise, most other revolutions failed because of an absence of effective centralization, often simply because of it spontaneity and the absence of a lively and general democracy. These include the German Revolution, the Spanish Revolution, 1956 and 1968. In all of these examples the contradiction of the leadership in the wrong direction was resolved, either because the leadership itself became ruling as in Stalinism and did not want to admit its own mistakes, or because the leadership led the working class directly to its downfall, like social democracy, or because there was simply no unified and democratic leadership. The contradiction that is to be resolved in democratic centralism can only be set and resolved in a living dialectical process; the answers to the questions must be found in practice. Democratic centralism is not a formula, and if it is made into a formula, the contradiction of leadership results in wrong leadership from the start. The answer to the problem of democratic centralism in the revolutionary awakening at the beginning of the 20th century was the councils. The councils were a living product of the class struggle. Today they are only a fetish of the left and that at a time when the productive forces have advanced so far since then. Like the councils, the party was based on the principle of delegation. Even without the bureaucratisation of the party, its bourgeoisisation and the democratic standstill in the country after the revolution, the principle of delegation was a more pragmatic than ideal "dissolution" of the contradictions of leadership. The principle of delegation, as well as the fact that it is now hopelessly out of date, is a principle that fluctuates strongly in the direction of centralization. It is therefore surprising that even some anarchists extol this principle. The current communication technologies have already solved the problem of centralization to a large extent and this would be a reason to look for new forms of organization instead of trying to revive the old ones. In any case, democratic centralism does not mean complete unity of action and opinion in all conditions. In spite of this, this is the idea of most Leninist groups. The other extreme, complete democracy or anarchy with no unity, is partly extolled by some anarchists, with others advocating some form of informal hierarchy or informal leadership. Both are views that either will not produce necessary leadership or will produce some informal kind of Stalinism, if any.

VII. On democratic centralism

Democratic centralism developed on the basis of the dynamic situation in Russia, first the weak democratic centralism in the party, i.e. unity in action, but freedom of external criticism, whereby the second point was directly defended and enforced by Lenin, later a strong democratic centralism arose, that means unity in action and in opinion, with freedom of criticism only inwards. Despite the fact that democratic centralism dynamically changed according to conditions, it has now become a sacred principle on the Leninist left. Even the most unorthodox groups practice it, and it practically causes the fragmentation of the Leninist left, for even the slightest difference in tactics and program means a division between groups and from one group into two. The insistence on democratic centralism is also one of the main reasons for the incompatibility between the Leninist and the non-Leninist left. Democratic centralism was certainly a factor in the establishment of the Stalinist dictatorship and helped Stalinism to establish and consolidate. Democratic centralism will continue to pose a threat to the democracy of society, even if all other factors are removed, and will be a factor that helps bureaucratization to establish itself. Because unity of action and opinion causes a homogenization of the labor movement, if such organizations will be the dominant ones in the movement and if the right communist party will be the dominant one in society, it will practically mean a ban on discussion outside the party. The party will then be the only place for free discussion and if this quality of the party disappears, which in turn can happen through international pressure and renewed bureaucratisation, free discussion in society will become impossible.

The contradiction between Leninism and anti-Leninism will be solved by the Leninists abandoning strong democratic centralism and by both sides meeting at the middle in two questions: on the question of centralism and decentralism and on the question of party or union/council. The middle between centralism and decentralism is both central and decentral planning. Markets must be abandoned, because even in a communist society they will cause economic stratification of the working class and therefore unequal distribution of power. But planning must be restructured after the experience of Soviet overcentralized planning. Planning will be centralized in as much as it will be done on one central digital platform, but it will be decentralized as it will happen in the individual cooperatives. The middle between partisanship and unionism, or council communism is achieved through the keeping of the party structure and the party as the moving force in the transitional period, but a less centralized one, but also by adhering to councils and to the principle, that the party cannot overtake the councils or unions or control them, like it happened in Stalinism. The party or parties (there can be also several communist parties in a single country) are still needed in the transitional period, because they have to prevent the return of capitalism and of support for capitalism in a period of crisis, which will surely come after the revolution and after a possible civil war. Both of these compromises are less ideological and principled and more pragmatic, as they meet in the middle of the two tendencies. Doing the opposite of what Stalinism did on centralism and the party can seem like the right thing to do, but it isn't, because undercentralization can be harmful for the revolution, mainly when it comes to questions of army organization and working without a party leaves us without an organized force to guide us in the whole process. The Stalinist left in non-Stalinist countries isn't anymore a danger to the revolution and a source of future Stalinism, because Stalinism wasn't caused by the ideology of Stalinists or Bolshevists for that matter, but by material conditions, most of which are not anymore present in most countries. The anti-Stalinist left should therefore be content with cooperating with the Stalinist left. However in some countries the Stalinist left cooperates with fascists and the far right and expresses reactionary positions on social issues, which is why in these countries it should be opposed.

VIII. On the division of labor and the petty bourgeoisie

The division of labor and, above all, the division into manual work and intellectual work played a very important role in the first development of class society. The development of the state was connected with the development of a coordination center for the production of irrigation systems and with the production of the first handicraft products, this coordination center was fueled by intellectual work. The problem of coordination is the reason for the development of the manager's work, and this in turn is one of the reasons for the development of the classes. From the beginning, the development of writing had the task of coordinating production and trade and distributing the surplus product. As soon as there was surplus product, trade and money developed. With that the bourgeoisie began to develop as the merchant class. Priests, the forerunners of philosophers and scientists, were first engaged in the procurement of medicine and in the organization of rituals and the protection of common property; only later did the church develop as the ideological defenders of class society, as the ideological state apparatus. For almost three thousand years, intellectual work only served the production of ideology that served the respective ruling class of the respective class society. Until recently, however, ideology was not so important for the preservation of class society, because the repressive state apparatus was the main basis for the preservation of class society, but ideology becomes the main base for class rule in late capitalism. Intellectual work increases in importance with

106

automation and it is very important at the end of class society, in the era of full automation and AI. In Stalinism, the division into intellectual labor and manual labor played a major role in the establishment of the bureaucracy and in the capitalist restoration by the bureaucracy, as in the Eastern Bloc, as in China. Above all, it was artists, scientists, technicians and managers who formed the bulk of the bureaucracy in the Soviet Union, who almost restored capitalism in the 1920s, and who then supported and ultimately enforced capitalist restoration in the 1980s.

The petty bourgeoisie is the part of the population that, with the bureaucratization of social democracy and Stalinism and with full automation, benefits most from the division of labor into intellectual work and manual work. As already mentioned, most of the party members were petty bourgeois in the 1920s and they then formed the majority of the bureaucracy. The Petty bourgeoisie is the greatest threat to a communist society, they threaten to become the new ruling class and they will become the greatest agent of capitalist restoration when communist society in some countries comes under international pressure or when communism finds itself in crisis.

IX. On bourgeois Marxism

Bourgeois Marxism is Marxism that is kidnapped by the bourgeoisie for bourgeois purposes, that is, to maintain bourgeois society. These purposes can be carried out consciously or unconsciously. Despite the statements of its followers, its content is dogmatism. This is treating Marx's work as a holy book and only as a book, not as the living, dialectical process that Marxism is. This dogmatism ultimately develops in two directions: anti-dogmatic dogmatism or dogmatic anti-dogmatism. These two basic currents of bourgeois Marxism can be simply described as Stalinism and postmodernism. At the same time, bourgeois Marxism begins to see Marxist theory as a fixed system that can be properly applied to any situation and any period. As soon as bourgeois Marxism begins to recognize contradictions in Marxist theory and between reality and Marxist theory, it splits into two currents: while some stubbornly stand on the "Marxist" theory and change their perception of reality, others go to the opposite extreme or reject the most important parts of Marxist theory, mostly to replace them with reformism, objectivism, subjectivism, or relativism. Both theories in their development stop at the point where they become objective and subjective bourgeois theories, that is, theories that support and sustain bourgeois society. Marxism should not be understood and interpreted as a formal system, the concepts and conclusions of which are immutable and unrelated to the dialectical level on which they were written, or not at all as an error-free system. Marx was only human and, moreover, could not finish his theory. Marxism is therefore incomplete from the start. The true dogmatism and the essence of Marxism is criticism for the purpose the revolutionary change in society. The mistakes and contradictions of Marxism are precisely evidence that a dialectical process exists, that is, evidence that it was a living process. The essence of Marxism is to promote this dialectical process. This is and remains the freedom of Marxism.

The grossest errors concern three main areas: the theory of the state, the theory of base and structure, and the theory of communism. In the theory of the state one can find the biggest and worst mistakes that have already caused the most practical mistakes or rather catastrophes in the last century. The difficulty in interpreting this theory lies in the fact that there is no real systematic theory. Marx wrote very little about the state and almost always in a specific context. Engels' theory brings us something that comes closest to the theory of the state, but also something that is incomplete and in part contradicts modern anthropological knowledge. In this theory, the state appears to be the product of the emergence of a class society and comes to the fore when it comes to protecting private property. In reality, however, the creation of the state was a little more contradictory and ambivalent process. The creation of the state went rather in parallel with the development of private property and, in some respects, as a predecessor of private property. The necessary conditions for the development of private property, that is, agricultural production, the existence of the family as an economic unit, and the accumulation of surplus products, were given before the state was fully developed. The state was originally used to protect common property and was later transformed into an institution promoting and protecting private property. However, this did not happen the same everywhere. India and China are good examples of the state becoming a major exploiter, while the development of private property, and thus stratification within agriculture, has been a problem for it and threatened its hegemony. This was particularly true of China, the Roman, and the Byzantine Empires. What does that mean? This means that our conception of the state in its dialectical development must be understood as a fetish. This also means that the state played a smaller and at the same time larger role in the development of class society. Above all, however, this means that the proletarian state alone cannot realize communist society. The state can at most be a tool, albeit a powerful one, for the development of communism. This is one of the main mistakes that caused Stalinism and the transformation of Stalinism into an extremely reactionary capitalism. Finally, the lack of a theory of the state, democracy and the dictatorship of the proletariat (as well as a misunderstanding of the dialectics of these concepts) brings us another feature of the rise of Stalinism: that is a formal and vulgar understanding of the proletarian state. For a state to be proletarian, it is not enough just to defend communist property and fight for it. If state property automatically means communist property, Marxism has no logic. It only makes sense if the surplus value of this society is completely redistributed to the proletariat and if the proletariat can rule this society legally, formally and realistically. Both were not fully realized in Stalinist societies. It was this combination of three misunderstandings of the state and the normative concept of the avant-garde that caused the rebirth of Stalinism into capitalism.

The problems of the transition from a class society to a class society can also be seen here. These problems can be illustrated by the problem of the base and the structure. The theory of base and structure is one of those parts of Marxism that is built on water. Basically there is only one quote that deals with this topic, and that quote is also very vaguely written. However, the relationship between the base and the superstructure can be illustrated very well by the relationship between nature and spirit in Hegel's logic. The superstructure always thinks that it is completely independent, but it is always just a product of its base. However, this base does not exactly determine the logic of the superstructure, and therefore there is a certain separate logic of the superstructure. This logic of the superstructure also determines the dynamics of class society, and therefore it is possible that the superstructure sometimes conflicts with the base, while the base also conflicts with the superstructure. A change is only possible because of these contradictions between and within these elements. The correct transition theory must therefore see and understand the dynamics of history and the contradictions between base and superstructure. A superstructure that has no real base is doomed to death, as is a base without a superstructure. The Soviet experiment failed precisely in the long-term contradiction between base and superstructure and therein, that is, in the contradiction between the formal socialist state and the real anti-socialist economy and at the same time in the superstructure itself in contradiction between the formal ideology and the real ideology of the party, the apparatus and the population. The anti-democratic character of the Soviet state led precisely to its anti-socialist character and vice versa. It was the rule of the party, or rather the rule of the unelected party leadership, and not the rule of the working class. The transition to a classless society is therefore misunderstood not only in Stalinist theory but also in anti-Stalinist theory due to dogmatism. Not only with Trotskyists but also with anarchists, the confusion of concepts remains along with the misunderstanding of their dialectical essence. The understanding of the concept of the state remains the same for both groups, with the exception that while anarchists view a state only as a bourgeois state and do not understand its need for the organization of production, Trotskyists still argue that the proletarian state is not democratic in the bourgeois sense has to be, does not have to be directly democratic and that only a proletarian state can build communism. The same views persist in transition theory. Despite the fact that Marx wrote his criticism of the Gothic program in his dialectical environment and the concept of the state remains unclear, anarchists on the one hand still deny the necessary first phase of communist society (assuming automation does not come before communism) and on the other hand Leninists suggest that the first phase of communist society presupposes the existence of money, the market, or that lack of value automatically presupposes communist society.

Another characteristic of bourgeois Marxists is therefore to relativize Marxist theory in both directions or to ignore its contradictions and obsolescence. One possibility is to relativize subjectivist aspects in Marxist theory that cause great difficulties, such as the necessary costs for the reproduction of labor, the realization of market values, the equivalent exchange, the role of market prices in the distribution of surplus value, and make the Marxist theory into a purely objectivist theory, which makes little sense in the analysis of today's capitalism, or they try to relativize the objectivist aspects of capital theory and convert it into a bourgeois theory. This transformation takes place mainly in two places: first, in value realization, where these subjectivists claim that value is fully realized in the market and therefore does not exist outside the market, and subsequently that the value of labor as well as exploitation and the added value can be realized on the market, with the consequence that exploitation cannot be counted outside of the market prices and only after these, with the consequence that loss-making companies do not exploit, just as companies in colonies do not carry out colonial overexploitation, and with the consequence that the market is responsible for successful exploitation; In other words, exploitation does not exist objectively in capitalism. Together with determining the cost of labor in the market or social determination, determining the value in the market and unemployment with no value, it means that without the market we have no way of determining exploitation and, secondly, no way of how to objectively determines the surplus and determine the contribution of each employee to the total surplus (which means equal pay for equal hours). The absence of bourgeois law only makes the first phase of communist society unnecessary, and without bourgeois law one of the great engines for the development of the productive forces is lost (with the result that civil law also requires a market and a law of value) . Both currents refuse to interpret Marx's theory as insufficient and to modify it to make sense, to be acceptable to today's bourgeois society and to be a theory that communist society can follow. The current trend, on the other hand, is not in the direction of being a dogmatist in the Marxist program, but of being a dogmatist in the Marxist theory of value.

The term "capitalism" shows us perhaps what is currently the best of left confusion about predictions of the future. Since

Marx as a capitalist only referred to a society in which there is competition and the law of value and the production of goods, they cannot imagine a post-capitalist society that will not be a communist society. The concept of "capitalism" could not originally refer only to a society in which there was "perfect" competition, nor could it rule out that the development of the capitalist production process took place in feudalism, nor could it exclude capitalist accumulation only in capitalism. This is due to the dialectical development of reality and concepts. The terms lose their meaning and justification according to the dialectical development. For example, it is very possible to imagine a "capitalism" in which because of automation most manufactured goods are not produced by human labor (or if this leads to enormous wage inequality, which is completely legitimized in the subjectivist classical theory) and simultaneously with a market, market prices and accumulation. One can also imagine a society that works partly or predominantly in slave labor, but in which there are still market prices and accumulation, so one can also imagine a society in which the market has practically disappeared and production is fully planned, but market prices and accumulation still exist, or a society in which the monopolies and the state are identical or closely related. Not only is it easy to imagine, but a hybrid society with these characteristics awaits us if there is no communist revolution in the next hundred years. Elements of such a society can be observed in Lenin's theory of imperialism and historical fascism.

Postmodernism changes the epistemological and ontological approaches to Marxism in a way, in which the universalist ambition of Marxism is stopped and Marxisms main theories, like historical materialism and dialectical materialism, or

114

the theory of value, are abandoned. Postmodernism also combines these theoretical abandonments with an abandonment of the revolutionary axiom of Marxism. Postmodernism also offers reactionary thinkers and reactionary thought a way out of the axioms of the Enlightment, which necessarily lead to Marxism and through relativism, constructivism and subjectivism offer to reactionary thought more grounding and more internal coherence. Postmodernism was a reaction to Stalinism and in the pursuit of correcting the mistakes of Stalinism it went to the other extreme and abandoned Marxism alltogether. Postmodernism has to be abandoned for a return to Enlightment ideas, best represented in orthodox Marxism.

X. What is communism

The main reason for the failure of Stalinism and thus also for the failure of communism lies on the ideal level in the difference between the economic and the social definition of communism and in the use of the economic definition of communism for Stalinism. Stalinism calls itself socialist because it has abolished capitalist exploitation and because it has socialized the means of production, but it does not see that it is threatened by the contradictions between the bureaucracy and the proletariat. It does not see that it functions and acts in a completely anti-socialist manner on a social level, it does not see that he is suppressing the proletariat and is not granting them the rights of co-determination it deserves. Simply following the economic definition blinds it to the impending collapse and uprising of the proletariat. It is a great paradox and a great tragedy that the only "Marxist" states have succumbed to a democratic uprising of the proletariat. The history of the Soviet Union and the Eastern Bloc teaches us that if communism is to be successful, then it must also be democratic and must not subdue whole populations and masses of peasants into communism and suppress them.

The further question is whether communism is the movement towards communism, or just the finished communist society. The anti-communists have become famous for calling every communist movement communism, although the Stalinists were known for being very careful not to call their own society communist. Answering this question is irrelevant and the answer to it is irrelevant, only depending on the currently advantageous tactics in propaganda.

Regarding the question of the first and second phases of communist society, it should be said that the first phase must be accelerated so that the second phase is ready for the creation of the AI, because for the equality between humans and the AI it is very important that there is communist exchange. This will likely be very difficult and we will likely have to move on to the second phase without our productive forces being developed enough, however automation may be able to solve this problem.

XI. Addition to the theory of value

Much has changed since the time in which Marx lived. The totality of the concept has changed, so it is not surprising that the concepts in Marx's writings appear outdated, incorrect and contradictory. Marxism itself was not ended by Marx in his lifetime, that in the theoretical form. Marx himself was a person and therefore flawed, so it is not a disparagement or elevation to say that he was wrong about certain things, not at the core. This contribution is intended to partially fill these holes. Labor has value measured by the use value it produces and increases through increased productivity, i.e. through machines. But the value of the labor remains the same. This enables a shift of the capital and thus the workforce to areas with low productivity, which means a lower level of automation. And the capitalist is not always a perfect capitalist.

If the work has no value, the whole system makes no sense as soon as you get to automation and really should divide the work fairly and efficiently in terms of productivity. It also makes no sense, because prices almost never reach or stop at exchange value and because prices are supposed to have an objective basis, but this cannot be objective in every world and is simply set in Marx, with the concept of value in other places represents something else, namely exchange value. This exchange value, however, is not objective in the previous sense, but depends on the social acceptance of certain norms that bring about the exchange that is supposed to be equivalent. The problem that this other conception opens up, however, is the determination of a quasi-objective use value, its comparability and the assurance that this does not lead to further classes or stratification. Because if one measures earnings, that means how many means of consumption is someone entitled to purchase in bourgeois exchange, by produced use values, one very quickly falls into extreme inequalities, for example according to how a specific use value is measured (one could say the use value of Marx works was unbelievable) and then whether one pays the use value in the earnings, although it is only a side effect, for example with different weather conditions or in the case of increased productivity through machines. The solution that comes to mind at the moment is purely theoretically to create the exception rule for intellectual work in the first phase of communist society and also retrospectively, where communist exchange applies to intellectual work. In addition, you have to create an objective, which means fair but agreed way of determining the use value, so that, for example, it is not possible, in the case of works of art, for example, that a picture has an incredible amount of use value, or only so much that no castes can be formed from it, further agree that side effects such as weather, climate or non-self-induced increases in productivity, such as with automation, are not included in the earnings.

XII. On the sharing economy

1.a. Reasoning: The "Sharing" economy is the "privatization" of existing open spaces and "free activities". It is "communism" according to capitalism. It takes advantage of the efficiency of common consumption and production as well as the advantages of the "free market" and combines them into a capitalist monopoly shell. The basis of the sharing economy is the market space fee. The "market" as such, the digital space as a better space than the real one and its possible replacement are owned and made a monopol by these companies.

1.b. In detail: The emergence of the sharing economy is in the time of an increasing number of monopolies, expansion of finance capital, high productivity and a relative "well-being" of the employees with a simultaneous reduction in the rate of profit. The aim is to reverse positive developments and strengthen negative ones. The reversal of positive developments, i.e. increased well-being - a large amount of personal property, knowledge, skills and remaining independence for the workers - is supposed to happen mainly through the "totalitarian" privatization of new spaces. In some areas this means right from the start the ownership of goods of these companies and their shared use by customers (car sharing), in others the use of personal property, so that it has only in this company its productive meaning (delivery service, Uber), in others it means the creation of a monopoly space for the exchange of personal property or "individually" manufactured goods (airbnb, "sashe"). The aim is to gradually eliminate the relative independence of workers and their collective organization through the gradual "privatization" of personal property, from automobiles to toothbrushes, and through complete individualization and control of their production and consumption. The increase in the rate of profit is achieved both through the complete destruction of the collective action of workers, through the exchange of producers, either through monopoly power, individualization of production or through the combination of both, and through the creation of monopoly prices and resources to increase value at the points mentioned - Monopoly of the exchange space, production space and ownership of goods. The aim of this project is to bring what previously could not be controlled in "real space" completely under monopoly control, and its incomplete control only took place after a thousand years of effort and violence. From the beginning a "market" is supposed to arise under the (full) control of capitalist monopolies.

2. a. The advantages of this diffuse sector can be summarized as follows: More efficient division of the means of production and consumption, either in personal or "monopoly" property. Complete reduction of "redundant" working hours due to space-time and the opacity of "reality". The use of the "free market" leads to low prices, competition and the development of "technology", of course to the detriment of the "space users". Firstly, it means the continued privatization of nature and the "commons" - common property or space, it also means the privatization of natural phenomena and the economic benefits of these phenomena, such as B. more economical co-consumption and co-production. This economy, that is, the difference between

121

this and the previous mode of production and consumption, will ultimately be a monopoly as an asset or a source of profit. Secondly, it means the centralization and "rationalization" of space-time and humanity in their communication and exchange - this should clearly be done in one place under the control and supervision of monopolies. This not only reduces the working hours caused by the opacity and lack of a center, but also reduces the free space for other forms of communication, exchange, production and consumption. These monopolies have the power to completely control communication, exchange, production and consumption. The free market - on the one hand, creates an inequality between monopoly and private users right from the start, with full competition on the part of users leading to low prices, little or no individual profits and complete individualization. On the other hand, on the monopoly side, there is no market, no competition, and the company can impose as high a price as possible, thereby "taking advantage of" users while taking advantage of central organization and communication, hard power, and the control of communication - and "user" activities at the monopoly remains. The goal is "perfect asymmetry" - a perfect class relationship in which one person knows, sees and organizes everything, the other cannot see, hear, or know and cannot do anything alone.

Practice: 3. a. Let's create alternative "sharing" platforms which, which do not have all the class properties of the capitalist sharing economy. It is important that they are not dictatorial monopolies, but are from the beginning under the "economic" control of the "users" and at the same time protect these spaces from attacks and transformations from capitalist monopolies, for which certain fundamental decisions must be defended and under control of this space. These fundamental decisions are the main focus of these areas on the anti-monopolistic, democratic and non-profit model where the value created by these spaces belongs to its users - as in a common fund. Another fundamental decision is to develop these spaces into spaces that go beyond the "free market" and personal ownership of consumables and means of production. While they initially create space for personal and "cooperative" production, consumption and exchange, with the help of a common fund in this area they will gradually create a favorable space for the expansion of joint production and consumption in this area. Specifically, this means at a later point in time shared cars for car sharing, shared apartments, shared different objects for use and production. At the same time, this "free market" must be controlled from the start so that it does not become a source of profit for people and companies outside of the space and for large inequalities within space. This requires some price control over the "cost of production". This space would include two economic models and three economic groups. The first space, which will be created later, but which will later form the basis of the project, is the exchange space within the community for a specific community "currency" based on time. The prices for individual goods and services are set democratically, otherwise set rationally, i.e. they should cover the production costs (for goods from outside the project). The second area, which would represent a chronologically first basis, is the area of the exchange of money between the means of production and consumption, but with the already mentioned partially controlled prices. The second group consists of money exchange between community members. The third group will be casual money exchange with non-members.

3. b. What matters is not the legal side of the company, but its true form. Therefore, it could also be a private company from the start, but at the same time with decisive basic decisions and prepared democratic structures on this platform from the start. The economic model could be similar to that of private companies, i.e. flat-rate (percentage) fees, with the profits possibly deposited in a common fund or returned to the users. What is exchanged, produced and consumed? There are different possibilities (several possible platforms) whether it is an exchange, a consumption or a production or what means there will be. The first and second questions depends on the input "capital" (either in money or in labor), i.e. on the field of activity and the value of the funds. Let us therefore initially rely on the smallest possible capital and the smallest possible scope.

"Bazaar" for rent in the style of Uber - UbiShare

In this case, it is possible to circumvent the difficulties with the value of the funds if, as in the case of capitalist sharing platforms, the personal property of the workers is used. In this case, this platform "only" offers space for the exchange and consumption (production is more capital-intensive and organizationally more difficult) of everyday objects. Specifically, this means a place for car rental with a complete reduction in the necessary working time for this exchange and without the need to enter into individual contractual relationships. The scope of this exchange (rental) can be extended to any production and consumable item. The time required for the execution of this rental agreement should be reduced as much as possible so that the assignment of an item takes several minutes, so that the payment, the prices for each rental agreement are not required and no individual communication and negotiation, meeting and even personal sale of the item is required (instead of being handed over in stores, possibly locked by the platform if registered users track objects and users and thus have the security of ensuring their own warehouse and free access for users later). These activities should be regulated by the platform and reduce the time for the individual rental. The rental itself, without transporting the object, should take a minimum amount of time. The platform's scope of activity could be expanded or include sales of production and consumables from the start. The rental and use of "cooperative" or "communal" items that are jointly owned by the association and that could be rented in the community for community "currency" or cash should be encouraged and preferred. At a later date, "shared" warehouses (funded by a joint fund or on the initiative of individuals) should be encouraged, especially for less valuable items that are freely accessible to the community and available to users outside the community. Such less valuable items can in particular be electrical devices or items that are usually not used in personal property. Access to such a warehouse could potentially be granted to users outside the community in the form of a flat fee. Depending on the level of activities and resources on the platform, many possible platforms can be created, combined or focused on one activity or "sector" of resources. The offer of these platforms can range from vehicle rental and rental consumption to the production of all possible consumables and means of production. It is also possible to combine non-monetary exchanges with monetary ones. In non-monetary areas, care must be taken to control reciprocity to avoid platforms like couchsurfing, where almost everyone treats the service as free (i.e. exchanging cash only for the community and doing this exchange with internal currency that cannot be accumulated etc.). It is also possible to create platforms for the exchange of services which, unlike Uber, Foodory and other delivery services, do not exploit their "users" and do not represent capitalist monopolies. Exchange platforms, on which private producers exchange their products, can also function democratically and gradually develop into production communities and co-production locations.

You can donate here:
https://www.gofundme.com/f/ubishare/donate

XIII. On the communist economy in capitalism

The last feature that distinguishes some currents on the left margin is either a revolutionary or an evolutionary solution. Here, Fourier and Marx traditionally face each other. This opposition is portrayed in such a way that Marx is in favor of a revolution at all costs and against all reforms, but Fourier and the anarchists only want to build socialism gradually from below. The truth is a little different, however, and that is, Marx was never opposed to reform and considered the revolutionary path necessary, not desirable. He ridiculed Fourier for believing that capitalists would never provide workers with more capital than just for survival. As is well known, this did not presuppose the emergence of modern social democracy and wages that would enable workers in imperialist countries to live in relative prosperity (compared to Manchester in 1840). Therefore, he says nothing about the combined tactic, at least in the imperialist countries, which will at the same time build a socialist sector and see a revolutionary clash as necessary. Many attempts at revolution have so far failed precisely because they succumbed to sabotage and economic blockade. In other words, because they had no socialist basis, they concentrated on the superstructure. Of course it is not possible to build a socialist sector in large industries and in competition with large monopolies, but perhaps where relatively small capital is needed, where competition is low or where there is no competition yet, i.e. in new markets and innovations. The digital market and the sharing economy seem to be particularly passable, where only intermediate platforms need to be set up. In particular, there should be cooperatives between producers and consumers. In these areas, socialist companies can even have a competitive advantage because they do not insist on high spending. Sectors with a low level of trade union organization are also preferred (since socialist companies function democratically and thus replace trade unions), such as restaurants and other services. The socialist sector should ideally function self-sufficiently, i.e. without contact to the capitalist sector, only if this contact is very advantageous for the socialist sector. Therefore, from the start it should contain a closed system consisting of the following parts:

1. Start-up platform: A platform where people and capital can be found to start a cooperative or social enterprise, both via their own social network and via crowdfunding.

2. Planning platform: Here consumers can plan and record their consumption and then plan production, also with a shared club card.

3. Trading platform: An online shop for cooperative production with its own delivery system, each with a means of transport, can register as a supplier.

4. Its own cryptocurrency, which can be used in this sector and set fixed prices for all goods, fixed exchange rates and progressive exchange rates, also serves as a bank

5. Own "bank" - a social fund with which companies make profits, which, according to a vote, provides interest-free loans and

subsidies for social enterprises and interest-bearing loans for capitalist companies. The bank would take colonial overuse into account and give more support to the colonial countries.

These systems, in combination, should ensure a sufficient competitive advantage for the socialist sector. Member companies of the system would be uniformly identified, for example with a brand Sol or Commons.
At a later stage of development this system could be part of the so-called original socialist accumulation, i.e. to accumulate at the expense of capitalist accumulation, through its own progressive prices and interest for the capital sector.

Three types of socialist enterprise would make up the socialist sector:

1. Social enterprise - a company owned by society as a whole, with the exception of individuals whose main source of income is ownership of capital and whose income is in the top 10 percent. All profits go to the social fund. As everywhere, decisions about the company are made directly and democratically, in day-to-day management with an elected, revocable leadership with an imperative mandate. Alternatively without leadership.

2. Strong cooperative - legal form of a citizens' association, therefore they do not have to pay any income tax, profits are not redistributed, at least half goes to the social fund, the others stay in the cooperative. Ideally, no entry fee.

3. Weak cooperative - The cooperative in the legal form distributes less than half of the profit, at least one third to the social fund. It must be voted on by members, not on the amount of the share. Input share as low as possible, increasingly less proportional to the deposit, from double (?) the wages higher the same share for higher payments (? Everything open to discussion).

If they were internationally active, individual cooperatives could directly eliminate the exploitation of colonial power by introducing equal real wages worldwide. In this way they could also influence the labor market in colonial countries and steal entire professional groups from the market.

XIV. Of Planning in Communism

Leftists often argue about whether communism will have a market or whether production will be organized with a plan. The planning need not be imagined according to the Stalinist model, namely with a strong centralization on one authority and with direction from the center and from above. Planning can also be democratic and relatively decentralized, at least in the way that anarchists use the word decentralization. The first change from capitalism to communism is the opposite of today's immense inefficiency of capitalism and how it produces for needs. In the current system, production for demand is only made available indirectly, both after purchase on the "market" and after profit. In most capitalist societies, however, there is a large gap between needs and consumption, between consumption and purchase, and between purchase and production. These gaps ultimately lead to poor production efficiency in relation to demand. This means that a lot is produced, most is sold, most of it is consumed, while not all who need it have access to these products. The task will therefore be to precisely measure all production, all purchases and all consumption and, in other ways, to create consumer-democratic institutions, councils able to directly award the necessary products, their quantity and quality control. Production is based on required, actual and expected consumption. Depending on the type of goods, the difference between production and purchase can be minimized, either production on request (design of consumer advice), on order, after the purchase or waiting. This is decided on the basis of the basic characteristics of the goods:

how much time is needed for production, depending on the production location and transport time for consumption, how many people, where and how long is needed for production and transport. Simply put, where production and transportation will take a long time (complicated machines, long distances) or where products are naturally worn out, the overproduction or production for the expected consumption outweighs the problem. It is possible to further minimize the gap between purchase and consumption by measuring consumption before purchase, by more efficient use and the selling for the time of use. It will also be possible to increase the efficiency within the production between the individual parts. The result will be better use of resources and manpower while consuming the same amount. It is produced for consumption and additionally according to a democratic decision. In order to reorganize production as needed (to make work a necessity), it is necessary to maintain a surplus and production for consumption. This will be possible either through increased automation, increased productivity and efficiency, or simply through reorganization (probably a combination of all three).

The central plan also shows the reality of a unified plan simply given by production after consumption. It is primarily about the unity of information, the elimination of parallel research and production and the mutual information blindness of companies under capitalism. Planning should therefore not be understood as a rigid and dictatorial system of the previous regime, but as an information and organizational method that leaves the initiative at the place of production and primarily harmonizes consumption and production (instead through "market" mechanisms). The incentive effects of competition are replaced by direct control of the company by consumer and production councils and a welcome initiative from everyone in innovation and proposed changes. Above the plan, that is, above the consumption of society, there is complete freedom in the initiative of production (with the exception of capitalist production). It is questionable whether in a system that has a unit of information about consumption, exploitation and a universal currency during working hours, it will be necessary at all to convert all production enterprises into social ones. Really central companies will be central research institutes and social services, which are financed from the social added value, i.e. the individual labor tax. All social institutions, i.e. political and controlling in nature, will be fully transparent and officials can be recalled at any time.

XV. On extremism and the protection of the constitution

The extreme left as well as the extreme right are placed on the same level and in the same box by liberal democracies. While there is no truly coherent theory of extremism, it is mostly argued that both groups engage in political violence and are dangerous to society. However, the extreme left is less violent than the extreme right in every country and has not carried out any terrorist attacks at least since the RAF in Germany and since the anarchist attacks in the USA in 1919. If the extremism theory were correct, the extreme left would be just as dangerous to the liberal order as the extreme right, however the extreme left is usually agreeing with liberalism on social progress and opposes racist, anti-Semitic and sexist oppression and discrimination . The extreme left does not pose a threat to minorities, in contrast to the extreme right, which specializes in hatred against minorities. The extreme left also does not want to abolish liberal and civil liberties, they do not even want to abolish the right to property, because they only want to abolish the right to own the means of production, something that is not an abolition of a constitutional right, because in reality there is always a conflict between the property rights of the workers to their surplus product and the right of the capitalists to the surplus product. Consent to the exploitation by the workers is proven to be coerced by the economic fact that workers would otherwise starve to death and because they cannot do anything legal against the economic order, whereby the illegality of the exploitation can be attacked. The communist revolution means only the enforcement of the constitutional right to property of the working class. The constitution does not need to change as such, because communism is completely compatible with liberal democracy. Even if the extreme left opposes liberal democracy, they are in favor of deepening democracy and liberalism and are therefore not anti-liberal.

It is also untrue to claim that communism, translated as Stalinism, is just as bad as Nazism and fascism, or in some way comparable to fascism. Anti-communists like to say that communism killed more people than fascism, 100 million, but they do not consider that the 100 million were not killed in genocide but were accidentally killed. The Holodomor was not genocide, because neither the peasants as a class nor the Ukrainians as a nationality were deliberately targeted, what happened then was an ideological incompetence of the administration, because the Stalinists expected that collectivization would bring a great increase in agricultural productivity and have therefore increased the farmers' levy of grain so that when the increase in productivity did not come, the farmers did not have enough to eat. The bureaucracy is responsible for the famine insofar as it refused to immediately admit that its predictions were flawed and that it used the grain to industrialize the country, but it is not responsible for deliberately killing anyone. The famine in China was exactly the same scenario, and this explanation is therefore more coherent than the Holodomor's explanation. The famines as well as the terror within the party were there, and that is the most important distinction from fascism, that they were not based on a necessary ideological connection with Marx, but on the arbitrary ideology of Stalinism. Marxism is not inherently and ideologically a murderous ideology like fascism. This can also be seen in the fact that today's fascists want to repeat the genocide, although today's communists at least don't want to repeat the famine and terror in their own ranks. The communists are not as dangerous for today's society as the fascists, because the famines of the communists will certainly not repeat themselves, because labor productivity is much higher all over the world and there are hardly any agrarian societies left. You can see, therefore, that equating communists and fascists is just a really anti-communist tactic that is supposed to protect class society. Anti-communism, on the other hand, is responsible for many anti-communist genocides in South Korea, Indonesia and Latin America and together responsible for 2 million deaths. But one rarely speaks of the anti-communist ideology as a dangerous ideology, although this ideology poses a greater danger to humanity than any other ideology.

XVI. On terrorism

It should be clear to every Marxist that Marxism does not defend individual terrorism as today's Marxists in the United States defend it. Above all, however, and this applies above all to the anarchists, individual terrorism should not be carried out because it invites the repression of the state apparatus and escalates the violence of the state, whereby it is clear that in today's situation the left cannot win the game of violence against the state. Terrorism is colloquially understood to mean murder or attempted murder for political purposes, but in US and European law terrorism means any violence for political purposes. That is why the activities of Antifa in the USA are terrorism. Another reason why the anarchist tactics are detrimental to the left is that they escalate violence and we cannot win this game. Leftists have to play the game of nonviolence as long as the working class does not support political violence and win the working class on their side and only when they get the majority of the working class support for communism can they advocate for the revolution. Advocating for the revolution earlier and escalating violence is suicide for the left. However, one should also deal with the fate of Marxism and Stalinism and come to the conclusion that Red Terror was immoral and did more harm to the left than good. As already discussed in Chapter 4, one should advocate assimilatory, not annihilatory Marxism and accept the Christian practice of forgiving the sins of the bourgeoisie and the fascists, up to the most extreme case.

Terrorism that is illegal is terrorism that is carried out by private persons, but if we take the definition of terrorism, which is violence for political purposes, then there is also legal terrorism that is carried out by the state, which is what includes politics. It is therefore important to conquer the state and be therefore allowed to practice legal terrorism.

XVII. On the civil war in the USA

Current events in the US, such as the BLM movement, the murder of BLM supporters by a Conservative killer, Kyle Rittenhouse, and the murder of a fascist in Portland, show us that the US is headed towards civil war between the left and the fascists. This development is worrying. The peaceful arrest of the conservative murderer and the shooting of the anarchist murderer by the police shows us that the repressive state apparatus will act much harder on the left than on the right. At the same time, it must be said that the right currently controls the state. In addition, one shouldn't forget the fact that all conservatives and Trump supporters will feel threatened by the shooting of fascists and that in a civil war the whole right will stand up against the left. If we realize that the right has the most armed people out of 30 million Americans with guns, it should be clear to any leftist that we cannot win a civil war. The left should therefore avoid any escalation of violence and also not take guns with them to protests, only body armor.

XVIII. How to reveal infiltration

Other security measures for activists will not be discussed in this chapter, for that look up *A practical security handbook* on the Internet. This handbook describes the available measures against infiltration, but they all rely on suspicions and are unreliable and don't eliminate infiltration for good. The reliable way of uncovering infiltration has to be done with the voluntary suspension of privacy for a security commission in every organization. This instruction is to be applied against new members, to securely check existing members, there has to be a process, where a security commission will be either selected by vote or volunteering, which will go through the audit through the surveillance from the whole group, after which the security commission will check the remaining members of the group. In this first audit, one has to guarantee that the audited members don't have bank accounts or smartphones the group and the commission doesn't know about, because every possible infiltrator will be notified by the group about the audit process. Another more secure way of securing the existing group, which however invades the privacy more, is that all members will be audited by the whole group. With new members, you have to make sure, that the member does know he has to go through a security audit, but don't tell him, what the audit entails. The new member has to surprised at a good moment, when there is enough time for the first step of the audit, and his credit cards and bank cards have to be checked in his wallet, so it can be ensured, he doesn't have other bank accounts. Also important is to check the smartphone he carries is his primary or only smartphone and to check all smartphones he has access to. The smartphone has to be checked in this first step of the audit, first the informations, which are not secured by password, that is the phone has to be checked first for surveillance apps, which could alert the organization doing the infiltration about the audit, this can be done manually or by antispyware software, of which the app Anti Spy Mobile is the best. Then the unknown calls have to be identified by Caller ID or some other similar software, then all the contacts have to be identified by the app Who, this can be also done later. In the next step, information has to be extracted from the phone with passwords, the most important are E-Mail and E-Mail contacts and telebanking. E-Mail accounts have to be examined closely. Facebook messages and friends have to be also examined closely and with E-Mail this has to be done periodically to check for encrypted messages. Income in the bank account has to be examined and it has to be examined, if the member works at the listed institutions or if these don´t serve as a cover for the state and other infiltrating organizations. The next step is to install on the primary and all smartphones parental control apps, like MMGuardian, Kroha, FamiSafe and TeenTime. These apps offer different features, so the best has to be selected according to the circumstances. Blocking websites and apps won´t be used against the audited member, the member will be only surveilled. Surveillance has to be done periodically and for a longer amount of time. The last step is to make sure with in-person surveillance, that the member doesn´t use a different smartphone or leaves the house without the smartphone. If this process is too time consuming, the audit of the bank accounts and income has to be prioritized, then the checking of E-Mail and Facebook and last surveillance. If leftists think, this will just lead to more information being given to the state and other organizations, this will be offset by getting rid of infiltrators. With the old methods of uncovering infiltration one can uncover it only when the infiltrator is sloppy or shows suspicious behavior. It is imperative, that this audit is applied to all members. This process can vary in organizations which don't have strict membership, however in such organizations it is imperative that the leaders and people dealing with sensitive information are audited.

XIX. On China

It has become a big phenomenon on the US-American left to portray China as a socialist society and the Chinese state as a proletarian state. To deny that China is a capitalist society one has to deny that a capitalist society is defined by the fact which mode of production is the dominant mode of production and one has to assert that bourgeois society is defined by the state. One then proceeds to claim that China is not ruled by the bourgeois, but even when the bureaucracy is ruling in China, that the bureaucracy is a part of the working class and that the working class can rule even through a minority of the working class. One has to deny that the bureaucracy is not part of the working class, that the working class is not defined by working for wages, that the bureaucracy can set their own wages and that the majority of the working class have to rule for the proletarian state to be proletarian. The Stalinist or Maoist explanation cannot materialistically explain the capitalist restoration in China, because it offers only an idealistic explanation (and this kind of idealism is not being accepted by this book). The Trotskyist explanation has to struggle with the contradiction, that the superstructure is Stalinist and a degenerated workers state, but the base is capitalist. Only the explanation, which asserts that the Stalinist society was a class society explains the capitalist restoration without contradiction, the only contradiction remaining being that the bureaucracy still calls itself Marxist. The only real contradiction would arise, if China managed to return to a Stalinist society and maybe also managed to wither away the bureaucracy. However this remains improbable.

XX. On anti-Semitism

Since the appearance of anti-Germans on the German-spekaing left, claims have spread that anti-Zionism is anti-Semitic, that Israel cannot be blamed for anti-Semitism because it is anti-Semitic, or even that any criticism of Israel is anti-Semitic. All of these accusations are false. Anti-Zionism is not necessarily anti-Semitic, even if it is mixed with anti-Semitism in the Muslim and fascist populations, because the right of the peoples to self-determination does not mean that every people has the right to build their own country in any country and to evict the local population. Zionism is a colonial movement and Israel from the beginning is a colonial project supported by British imperialism. Even if the expulsion of the natives before the Nakba was legal and was done by buying land from feudal lords, from the peasants' point of view it was expulsion. The fact that Israel was necessarily justified by the Shoah is also wrong, because the Shoah did not cause Israel to emerge and Israel would have come into being even without the Shoah and because Israel is not a safe home for Jews, because the Jews there are under constant threat, surrounded by anti-Semitic nations and countries. The Jews are certainly more existentially threatened in Israel than in the Diaspora, even if they do not experience social anti-Semitism in Israel. The threat to Jews posed by anti-Semitism and fascism will only end if anti-Semitism is ended in communism and only communism can provide this security for Jews. Only a great communist power like the Soviet Union was able to stop fascism, although too late for millions of Jews, but if fascism had triumphed over the Soviet Union, no Jewish nation would exist today. In spite of everything, Israel is responsible for a large part of anti-Semitism in the Arab world and less in the whole world, because the existence of Israel and the occupation of Palestine causes a huge amount of anti-Semitic sentiment, especially in the Muslim and Arab world. The criticism of Israel is also motivated by anti-Semitism, also in Europe, but not all criticism of Israel is automatically anti-Semitic. Although anti-Zionism would also be correct at the time of the establishment of Israel, despite the fact that most Jewish emigrants could only find shelter in Israel, anti-Zionism today, especially with the support of Fatah and Hamas, is in practical consequence a support for the expulsion of Jews from Israel and therefore anti-Semitic. A solution to the conflict would either be the establishment of a Palestine for Jews and Arabs, but under the supremacy of the Jews and with an ethnic army for the Jews, or a Palestinian state, which would however be disarmed and allow the Israeli army on the territory of Palestine, for the defense of Israel in a prospective conflict with the Arab nations. However, the reason for no solution in this conflict is Israel, which does not want to fulfill the Oslo Accords and because the right-wing government of Netanyahu plans to evict the Palestinians in order to be able to annex Palestine without losing the majority of Jews in Israel. All leftists, including anti-Germans, must reject such a solution.

XXI. For femininity

In today's society, masculinity primarily means two qualities and vices: pride and aggression. A majority of male activities are inherently reactionary and reactionary in their current practice. Manhood is so toxic that it cannot be cleaned up. Femininity, on the other hand, means empathy and tenderness. Everyone should therefore be feminine and femininity should be seen by the left as the solution to sexism.

XXII. For Christian Marxism

Although Marxism has traditionally been anti-theist, it should be clear from what has been said in this book that it is compatible with Christianity. The connection of Christianity with Marxism, however, creates many advantages, as for Christianity, also for Marxism, for Marxism above all the advantage that Marxists can connect with the existing consciousness of Christians and can use the Bible to their advantage. Although the Bible contains many reactionary elements, it also contains passages about communist property and a communal way of life among the early Christian communities. Also, the teaching of love, (temporary) pacifism and forgiveness are very beneficial components of Christianity for Marxism, because from a utilitarian point of view love, conditional pacifism and the teaching of forgiveness can avoid a lot of suffering and bring happiness and a Christian Marxism also will create much less resistance in the liberal and Christian western world.

[1] Lenin, IW: State and Revolution, Lenin Werke Vol. 25, Dietz Verlag, 1960, p. 417

[2] Trotsky, Leo: Revolution betrayed, 1936, 9.3. chapter

[3] Lenin, IW: State and Revolution, Lenin Werke Vol. 25, Dietz Verlag, 1960, p. 431

[4] Lenin, IW: State and Revolution, Lenin Werke Vol. 25, Dietz Verlag, 1960, p. 430

[5] Lenin, IW: State and Revolution, Lenin Werke Vol. 25, Dietz Verlag, 1960, p. 408

About the author

Michal Andrej Molnár is a student of philosophy and theater, film and media studies at the University of Vienna. He is a Marxist activist who is not a member of any organization.

You can contact the author on these pages:

Facebook - https://www.facebook.com/michalandrej.molnar
Twitter - https://twitter.com/an_molnar
Instagram - antistalefty
Email - mi.an.molnar@gmail.com
Academia.edu -
https://independent.academia.edu/MichalAndrejMoln%C3%A1r

www.ingramcontent.com/pod-product-compliance
Lightning Source LLC
LaVergne TN
LVHW051345050326
832903LV00031B/3748